Overcoming Common Problems

EDITOR'S ...

The books in th... help on a wide ra... we encounter in ...

The aim of t... convey what is kn... in a balanced and ... what help and re... hoped for and how problems can be better understood and made easier to live with. Each book has been written in a simple and direct style by a doctor with special knowledge in the field. It is hoped that the series will help the reader to realize that many other people have similar difficulties and as a result feel less isolated.

The first books in the series deal with hypochondria, sex, feelings about childbirth, and insomnia. It is intended to build up a comprehensive series covering a number of themes relating to common problems of modern life with the emphasis on practical help and guidance both to the sufferer and to those close to him or her.

DR ALAN KERR

[illegible] PREFACE

[illegible] series have been written to give [illegible] of common [illegible] which [illegible] everyday living.

[illegible] of the series is [illegible] [illegible] own and what [illegible] [illegible] [illegible] can be [illegible]

[illegible]

FEELINGS ABOUT CHILDBIRTH

Overcoming Common Problems

Other books in the same series

HYPOCHONDRIA
Dr F. E. Kenyon

INSOMNIA
Dr Peter Tyrer

SEX
Dr F. E. Kenyon

In preparation

SHYNESS AND ANXIETY
Dr Phyllis Shaw

STRESS
Dr Peter Tyrer

MID-LIFE CRISIS
Dr Brice Pitt

Overcoming Common Problems

FEELINGS ABOUT CHILDBIRTH

Dr Brice Pitt
M.D., M.R.C.Psych., D.P.M.

SHELDON PRESS
LONDON

First published in Great Britain in 1978 by
Sheldon Press, Marylebone Road, London NW1 4DU

Printed in Great Britain by
Richard Clay (The Chaucer Press) Ltd, Bungay, Suffolk

ISBN 0 85969 158 6

Contents

For Caroline and Rosalind

Author's Preface

I was scribbling furiously while queueing for a snack at the National Theatre, when an American girl behind me asked what I was about. I explained that I had to meet a deadline for Sheldon Press and that the subject of my book was 'Feelings About Childbirth'. She raised an eyebrow. 'How would *you* know?'

She had a point, I am the wrong sex ever to know just what it feels like to have a baby, though as a father I can share many of women's feelings about childbirth. My presumption in writing a book on the subject, however, is based mainly upon a research interest which has led me to interview well over a thousand women at different stages of childbearing and ask about their feelings. This book incorporates much of what they told me and what I observed, together with what I have read about the subject. I hope that the part played by masculine intuition is very small.

I should like to express my thanks to my obstetrician colleague at The London Hospital, Professor Peter Huntingford, for taking a lot of trouble to read through the manuscript and give me advice and highly constructive criticism, though the views expressed in the book remain very much my own. My thanks are also due to my secretary, Maureen Marshall, who converted my scrawl into a legible typescript. Finally I want to record my appreciation of all the mothers who participated in the research at The London Hospital for their tolerance, frankness and goodwill.

BRICE PITT

I

Mixed Feelings

In the days when sex and reproduction were referred to coyly, if at all, pregnancy was called 'an interesting condition' and childbirth 'a happy event'.

Pregnancy, however commonplace, remains a condition of great interest. (You probably would not be reading this if it were not!) There is the fascination of the biological miracle whereby the woman conceives and is transformed through the subsequent nine months into a more and more pregnant 'mother-to-be'. Not only is she changed personally—sometimes quite dramatically, more often subtly—but there is the promise of the baby she is carrying, which may be imagined to be special in all sorts of ways whilst its looks, temperament, talents and even its sex are as yet unknown.

'A Happy Event'? Well for many, most of the time, yes. To give birth to a wanted and planned baby is an occasion for joy and deep satisfaction. More often perhaps, conception is unplanned, but after early misgivings the baby is wanted and its birth is again welcomed warmly. Where unplanned and unwanted, however, the feelings are very different. Even today, when in most countries abortion is more available than ever before, too many children are born unwanted. It is unhappily not true that though the pregnancy is at first rejected the feelings towards the child always become positive if it continues to term. About a third of mothers who did not want their child in pregnancy do not want it after it is born. Depression and resentment are then unfairly, but understandably, focused on the hapless child.

Even when the pregnancy is much wanted, feelings

about conception may be mixed. There is a world of difference between wanting something and getting it, as those who get promoted, married, or even those few who win the football pools, discover. A greatly wanted, as yet unattained object is seen as an ideal. Once grasped, however, the reality is rather different. The snags are evident and a period of adjustment is required before the full implications of the achievement can be accepted.

It is human nature to have mixed feeling about those things which matter to us most. To those who wish that we would be logical and consistent, know our minds and see things in black and white, this can be thoroughly exasperating, but this is how people are. It is wholly human, for example, to feel hatred at times for those whom we love very much, because they have such power to hurt us when they withhold themselves from us and give their attention to others. We often feel guilty compassion for those we mostly hate, because we do not always want to feel that we can really harm them. It is altogether human to want quite opposite things at the same time.

This *ambivalence* is particularly striking in the field of *contraception*. Publicity, advice and contraceptive resources are more available now than ever before and yet the proportion of unplanned pregnancies is still almost fifty per cent. Is this to be explained by ignorance, or technical failures? Not altogether. It has been suggested that for some couples the contraceptive pill diminishes sexual desire because it is too effective! So often it turns out that the 'technical failures' are in fact human errors. Most often the reasons why the woman on the pill conceives is because she doesn't always take it. Again, sexual dissatisfaction following male sterilization (vasectomy) is sometimes explained when the operation is felt to be too final. The sheath, the coil, the diaphragm, the safe period and the 'withdrawal' method are more popular with many because there is a small but definite risk (not always that small in the case of the safe period and withdrawal method!) of conception.

Usually the first question I ask women referred to me because they are seeking an abortion is 'how did you get to be pregnant, then?' Frequently the retort I get is, 'don't you know the facts of life, doctor?' To which I reply, 'yes, don't you?' This (generally good-humoured) exchange leads to the disclosure of feelings which were rather different at the time of conception from those which predominate a few weeks (or sometimes months!) later. It is clear that forgetfulness and haste are often motivated. There is a desire to fall pregnant at the very time when precautions are supposedly being taken against doing so. Sometimes this is to cement the relationship with the sexual partner, where this seems to be at risk. Sometimes, especially in teenagers, there is an element of 'Russian roulette' to add extra excitement and offer the chance of a drastic change from a life which seems boring and sterile. Often too, there is a biological yearning to procreate, which thwarts the technical devices whereby civilization seeks to control its population. To my mind this fundamental ambivalence about getting pregnant will always to some extent bedevil family planning, however extensive education and foolproof the methods.

So even the woman happiest with her pregnancy has some misgivings, and she who appears most emphatically to reject the pregnancy may be doing so despite some wistfulness, as a tiny part of her wishes to have the baby. Most mothers-to-be come somewhere in between these two extremes, and their feelings are more equally mixed.

Motherhood is the purpose for which woman was created—or is it? Not long ago it was assumed that all women wanted to get married and have children (in that order!) and those who did not were pitied or mocked for being 'on the shelf' if they were not married, and somehow blamed for 'selfishness' if their marriage had failed to produce children. Attitudes have changed remarkably quite recently. Is it better to be a woman or a person first? Is it better to be a mother or to have a good job? Is mothering a good job? Is motherhood a fulfilment or a trap? Does the world need any more children anyway? To give up one's job in order to have a baby is to change one's role in society. Many women are only too eager to do so after many years of longing. Others may be less assured of the value of their new position. To be a mother may seem both the easiest and the most difficult thing in the world.

The physical requirements for begetting a child are well within the capabilities of most women. Some fall pregnant with the greatest facility, and the rearing of an infant comes as naturally and easily. Others are daunted by the responsibilities of motherhood. To the new baby, and throughout childhood, the mother is the most important person in the world, with tremendous capacity for good or ill. Not only is the baby totally dependent on the mother for its physical needs but the psychological effects of mothering have a major effect in moulding the personality. The ideal mother is mature, unselfish, intuitive—quick to recognize or anticipate her baby's needs and to put them first. To be so exceptional may seem beyond the powers of almost anybody!

Feelings are further mixed up during pregnancy by the major changes in the levels of hormones in the blood. Such changes affect most women during the menstrual cycle, rendering them depressed or irritable when the period is due. During pregnancy hormone changes are much greater, and consequently unexplained fits of depression and tearfulness, irritability, sensitivity, buoyancy and broodiness may be disturbing.

The spouse is often the object of mixed feelings. What is his attitude to the pregnancy? Does he really want it? Was it his 'fault' in the first place? Is he ready to be a father? (For the first time, or again?) Will the present harmonious twosome ripen into a family when the baby comes along, or will it be a case of 'two's company, three's a crowd'? How will he react to the changes in his partner's physical appearance, to the reduction in sexual activity and to the awareness that she is becoming a mother? When the baby arrives, will he be a tower of strength, or will he opt out?

Feelings about doctors and midwives are also frequently mixed. They are both trusted and suspected. Will they be nice, wise, helpful and understanding or will they be callous, uninformed and prejudiced? Is the hospital (usually) in which the birth is to take place a haven, or will it be a sort of glorified conveyor-belt where women are processed by remote gowned figures in an atmosphere of strange smells and alarming apparatus? Will the other women be comrades (all girls together) or will they be off-hand and bitchy?

Thus it is not surprising that for most women pregnancy is a time of considerable anxiety as well as eager anticipation. Childbirth may be experienced as intense fulfilment, or a nightmare, and for some the period after the baby is safely delivered is one of deep depression.

In the subsequent chapters these feelings will be examined in more detail, and the extent to which they arise from within, from past experiences which come turbulently to the surface at the time of childbearing, or result from happenings in the here-and-now of the mother-to-be's external life, her circumstances and relationships, will be considered. Ways of coping or coming to terms with disturbed and disturbing emotions will be explored. At the very least, even if answers are not always forthcoming, it is hoped that some mothers may be helped to feel more comfortable with their questions. Although the contradictions between feelings cannot always be resolved, some women may benefit from learning that it is quite natural and normal for them to be mixed.

2

Relationships

Three people are especially important to most pregnant women: her mother, her husband or sexual partner and the baby-to-be.

MOTHER

A lot of the 'unfinished business' which comes to the surface, particularly in the first pregnancy, concerns the woman's mother. The mixed feelings discussed in the last chapter are particularly strong for the person on whom there is at first total dependency. To the new born baby there is probably no distinction between herself and other people. All she will be aware of is comfort or discomfort, pleasure or pain—being well fed, warm, dry and held cosily, or being hungry, cold, damp or uneasy. Very young babies seem to express contentment mainly by sleeping, and distress and anger by crying. Their environment is either satisfactory or displeasing, calling forth feelings akin to love, or of hatred and rage. Some psychoanalysts believe that the discovery that the prime source of contentment—the mother—is also the source of discontent, when she fails at once to meet her baby's needs and relieve her suffering, is deeply disturbing and is, indeed, the origin of depression.

The developing baby first becomes aware of a part of the environment which is always with her—her own self. Then there is another part which is nearly always present—her mother. Then there are others parts which are pretty often in evidence—the father and other members of the family. So begins the awareness of other people, and the business of relating to them. The mother who is so much loved and needed is not always around to minister to her baby's needs. She sees to the father and to any other children, and perhaps leads her own life. Only gradually does the baby become aware that she cannot have everything she wants; that she is a very little person in a big world and that she has to wait for some things and do altogether without others. During this painful change from what Freud called 'the pleasure principle' to 'the reality principle' there is much frustration and resentment. To the very small child her anger is alarming. How is she to control an emotion which seems powerful enough to destroy others and even herself? It is rather like igniting a charge of high explosive: there is a fear of doing terrible damage, and of being damaged. If the mother is aware of the waves of hatred her child is feeling—and how should she not be?—her vengeance may be terrible. To the infant the parents loom very large and even though later in life they are usually seen as nearer to life-size, the impact of the mighty first impression continues.

Long after these problems of the *couple*, mother and child, 'the mother I love and need I have also hated and hurt so then she may hurt me', there are those of *rivalry*. In the first place there is rivalry with the father for the mother's undivided attention, and then with any brothers and sisters, particularly younger ones. Later still, as she becomes aware of her femininity, a little girl is envious of her father's love and attention to the mother and sometimes tries to take her place. This leads to guilt and the fear of punishment by the mother. All these very strong emotions are too much for most children to cope with in infancy, and they are for the most part repressed, or pushed away, into the unconscious mind. This means that they cannot be readily recalled—very few who read this book will remember having such stark feelings about their parents in childhood—but not that they are out of the way and have no further effect. Freud called the unconscious 'dynamic', meaning that conflicts which had been repressed and could not therefore be remembered, still had a considerable effect upon the growing and adult personality. All sorts of 'hang-ups' in later life probably result from this period.

The ideal way out of unresolved conflicts with the mother is by the process of *identification* during adolescence and early adult life. As she gets older the daughter feels for her mother as another woman in the same family and a closeness develops, as they share feminine interests, which off-sets the early antagonism. However this does not always happen. Some mothers are not so companionable, and some daughters' repressed feelings of guilt and hostility are too strong for them to be able to achieve any closeness.

Yet the pregnant woman in many ways needs her mother. In the first instance she needs her approval. Where feelings of guilt and rivalry are strong, there may be the question, 'is anyone else in this family allowed to have babies?' If the answer is not a confident 'yes' there may be a deep fear that the pregnancy will in some way be blighted; conception will not take place in the first place, or there will be a miscarriage, or the baby will be born abnormal or will not thrive or even survive after birth. In more obvious and practical terms the mother's support, especially during and after the baby's birth, is greatly needed. Reassurance about feeding and minor ailments from a trusted mother, and of course baby-sitting, are a tremendous help but where the fear of rivalry is very intense help freely offered may be suspect, lest the mother should make a take-over bid for the baby.

HUSBAND (OR LOVER)

Not every woman is a natural mother and certainly not every husband (or lover) is a natural father. Although the marriage service states that the purpose of the union is to beget children, not every couple weds with that aim foremost in their minds. It does not inevitably follow that wanting to be with another person means wanting to have a child. A couple is one thing, a trio, quartet, quintet or even more is very different. Whereas some couples feel incomplete without a family, others feel well content with each other. Or it may be that one wants children and the other does not. To share his wife with children and to be responsible for them himself is not every man's wish. Yet because of the vagaries of contraception mentioned in the previous chapter, many an unwilling man finds himself about to be a father. Even if he wants to be a father, or to father another child, he may not want to do so now. If conception takes place very quickly after marriage or after the birth of the last child, there may be dismay at the disruption of the original relationship with his wife, or further delay before its return.

Even when the child is wanted there are anxieties about the effect of pregnancy, childbirth and a baby on the mother and on his relationship with her. Will her health suffer? Will she go off sex? Will the baby come between them? Will she have used him as a kind of stud, to give her the baby, and then lose interest in him? How will he measure up to the responsibilities of fatherhood? Will he provide proper emotional and material support to his wife and child?

These anxieties are shared by his wife, who needs his support more than anyone else's, even that of her mother. His reaction to the news of the pregnancy, his behaviour during its course, his attitude to the birth, his involvement and his potential as a father are all possible causes of concern.

It is very unlikely that a rocky marriage is made more stable by having a baby. On the contrary, the demands of pregnancy and parenthood are such that the added strain may prove to be the final straw.

Unfortunately women's fears that their husbands (or

lovers—as so many couples these days live together without being married) will lose interest in them and opt out after the baby's birth are not altogether unfounded and although more and more husbands are actively interested in their wives' childbearing, many others are still inclined to leave them to get on with it and to change their own lives remarkably little after the baby is born. However it does seem that the more that the husband is involved with the pregnancy and the actual birth, the more helpful he is likely to be afterwards. The traditional and now outmoded image of the anxious father pacing up and down in the waiting room whilst his wife is giving birth, and then handing round cigars afterwards, was comical and belittling. Husbands who attend antenatal clinic with their wives and are present at her labour feel thoroughly identified and can be of the greatest help.

In some primitive societies there is a ritual called Couvade, in which, whilst the mother is giving birth in a hut attended by the women of the tribe, her husband goes through an elaborate public rite accompanied by elders. He imitates the act of labour with a great deal of noise and ceremonial dancing. This is to drive away evil spirits who are traditionally supposed to be abroad and looking for the opportunity to cause mischief at this critical time. One wonders though whether, in a male dominated society, this is not the means whereby the man keeps his end up in a situation in which his wife would otherwise have the limelight! In our society the term 'Couvade Syndrome' is sometimes used for the aches and pains which husbands have been found to be significantly more likely to suffer or present whilst their wives are pregnant. It is not surprising that abdominal pains should be the commonest, but less easy to explain why toothache is so much more troublesome at this time. The Couvade Syndrome is just one indication that the husband is much concerned in his wife's pregnancy and shares her anxieties.

THE BABY-TO-BE

At the beginning of pregnancy many women are more concerned with the fact of being pregnant, and the effect this will have on their lives, than with the actual baby to be given birth. Quickening, the moment when the baby's movements are first felt, is a most important development in the mother's relationship with her unborn child. For many, until this moment, the baby is more of an idea than a reality. For some, indeed, it is hardly more alive in its own right than one of the tissues of the body—a piece of gristle, say, or even a clot. But when these movements announce the baby's presence the mixed feelings about pregnancy are usually resolved and the mother's attention focuses on the temperament and character of her infant.

The greatest concern is that the baby should not be abnormal (see Chapter 5) and the commonest remark made when asked, for example, the sex preferred is 'so long as it's all right it doesn't really matter'. However, the baby's sex and other attributes matter, of course, a great deal. In some societies it is vital at least to start with a male baby. Poor Anne Boleyn would probably have kept her head if she had been able to give King Henry a male heir! In many cultures other than those of Western society a boy is hardly less important, as the inheritor of a masculine tradition. On the other hand, after a succession of boys many parents long for a girl, and sometimes requests of abortion are qualified by 'if I knew it was going to be a boy (or girl) it would be all right'. The mother may have more personal reasons for wanting a baby of a particular sex. She may feel more comfortable with girls and want one to be a companion with whom she can identify in an otherwise mostly masculine world. She may find men as strange in some ways as beings from another planet, and not know how she would cope with the responsibilities of bringing up a boy of her own. Or she may feel that as a woman she has taken second place all her life and that opportunities have been denied her because of her sex. She may then very much want a boy who will be able to do, almost on her behalf, all those things she feels bad about not having been able to do herself.

There may be particular difficulties with a particular child. For example, one woman I knew felt that she had been at a particular disadvantage as a second daughter, and she was very apprehensive in case her second child should be a daughter like her first, because she half expected that those old and painful difficulties would be revived in her child and she would not be able to cope with them.

Husbands, of course, may have very strong feelings about the sex of the child to be, wanting a boy to whom to be 'dad' and through whom to relive boyhood, or a little girl to cosset and adore for her dainty femininity. If he is at odds with his wife over this then there may well be trouble in store. The choosing of a name before the baby's birth often shows the various pressures there are on the unborn infant to be what various members of the family want. How many Lesleys and Hilarys and Geraldines were so called because the disappointment over having a girl is offset by giving her a neutral or feminized male name? Often names are chosen after key members of the family—*her* uncle, *his* mother—or after current celebrities, suggesting the rich fantasies and wishful thinking that are projected upon the unborn baby.

Some women, when they think of their baby, think of him or her only at a particular age. They think only of the helpless infant suckling contentedly and looking up at them with adoring eyes, or of a sturdy toddler full of vigour and forward for his age. Or they think of the schoolchild bringing credit to his or her parents. Or they may think as far ahead as university, his occupation or the comfort and support he may be in their old age. Not all these thoughts, however, are so positive. There may be fears of a bad or uncontrollable child who will show them up, or embody family failings in the way that notorious black sheep already have done.

It is good that the mother should anticipate the various stages of her child's life and that she should explore various possibilities, but in a flexible, accepting way. If she is heavily committed to one particular kind of child then really she is using that child to make up for her own disappointments or failed ambitions and she is going to have a lot of difficulty in seeing him or her as a separate person. The possibility that the child could be so many things is one of the most exciting features of pregnancy and one of the reasons why the pregnant woman is in some respects precious during these nine months and valued for more than herself, but it is likely to be an unhappy baby which has its role and future clearly mapped out before it's made its entrance into the breathing world.

3

Planned and Unplanned Pregnancies

Why *do* we want to have babies, or a particular baby at a particular time? There are, of course, several different reasons, but the most important must be the fulfilment of the powerful *biological drive* to procreate on which the survival of every species depends. (Cole Porter lists quite a few in 'Lets Do It!') The intense pleasure of sexual intercourse is a vital part of this biological urge, but so is a deep yearning to have children, which varies a good deal in different people and in the same person at different times, but tends to be especially strong, naturally, in women, during their childbearing years.

Although we are thinking and sometimes rational beings, this yearning is not always appropriate to the circumstances, so that the longing to have a baby may overwhelm practical commonsense objections to, say, having another so soon, or after so long, or before the car's been paid for, or when there really isn't enough room. Having the gift of speech we do our best to explain or 'rationalize' our desires, but really there is no need: it is the same irresistible force which compels salmon to swim up rivers against numerous hazards to spawn and die. As thinking, rational beings we may be irked to be so dominated by our instincts, but they have to be reckoned with. Certainly we have the wit and the technical means to plan our lives up to a point, but it is no easier to thwart our instincts altogether, than it is to dam a river without causing a flood.

Another fundamental (and perhaps uniquely human) reason for wanting a child, or children, and one which applies quite as much to men as to women, is the desire for a kind of *immortality*. As thinking, rational beings we know, unlike presumably the birds and the bees, that we are going to die. However real we seem to ourselves we know that we must, fairly soon, return to that oblivion from which we came (or to a necessarily unknown after-life), but in a sense we can live on for a few generations or perhaps for as long as humanity itself survives, through our children and our children's children. In our germ cells lies the hope of a lasting legacy to the world of a part of ourselves. Also an heir may be wanted to continue a family business, or to inherit an estate.

The beautiful, bewildering, ecstatic, agonizing state of being in love means idealizing one's partner and wanting to be wholly at one with him or her. This psychological fusion is perfectly but fleetingly expressed in sexual intercourse. To have a baby as the *fruit of one's love*, an offspring with an equal heredity from each, brings many couples still closer together. Not infrequently a baby is sought by one or other of a couple to bring them close again when they are drifting apart.

Various family and social pressures may be of importance. A baby may be planned because the parents' parents want or *expect a grandchild*, or because of *rivalry with brothers and sisters* who may have children. A man may wish to demonstrate his *virility*, a woman her *fertility*. In some cultures, e.g., Roman Catholic and totalitarian states as well as certain of the less developed societies, a couple are expected to procreate and *swell the numbers of their kind*.

Those who feel unloved often want a baby to love and *love them back*; the unsettled teenager, at odds with her parents, or the wife who feels neglected and unappreciated, may both seek an infant for this purpose. There may sometimes be an element of *insurance*. 'I want a child who will be a good son or daughter, and look after me when I'm old!' Quite often, unhappily, a pregnancy is sought not because a child is particularly wanted, but as a *means to another end*. A disturbed adolescent may wish to hurt her parents by getting pregnant; at the same time she may be acting out her rivalry with her mother, as a producer of children, and demonstrating that she is no longer a little girl, but properly grown up. A woman angry and disenchanted with her husband or lover may seek aggressively to inflict a pregnancy on him, while he, vengefully or to keep her under his domination, may try to do the same to her. Or, pregnancy may seem preferable to a course of study or a job which a woman is finding uncongenial.

However, with all these reasons, good and bad, for planning a pregnancy, almost as many, it seems, are *unplanned*. It isn't easy to be sure just how many, because some women are reluctant to admit that the pregnancy was unplanned, for fear of looking foolish or somehow putting a blight on the pregnancy by acknowledging that it was not intended (such superstitious thinking is extremely common at this time). When I was doing a survey at The London Hospital some years ago, though, 42 per cent of a random sample of women having their babies there admitted that they had not planned the pregnancy. Unplanned pregnancies are sometimes wholly unplanned and accidental, as when there is a failure in the contraceptive, or ignorance of proper contraception. Often though they are unconsciously motivated, as has been explained in Chapter 1.

An unplanned pregnancy is sometimes a pleasant surprise and instantly accepted. More often acceptance comes eventually after early anxiety and misgiving. But not infrequently the unplanned pregnancy is also unwanted, and a request for termination by *abortion* results. In most countries abortion is only allowed where continuance of the pregnancy is a hazard to the mother's health. This includes, under 'mental health', severe distress, and this is now the commonest reason for termination in Great Britain. On the whole women who really want an abortion are much relieved by having one, but those whose feelings are very mixed—adolescents, some dominated wives and those whose physical health is at risk—may react very badly. Assessment of the woman ostensibly seeking abortion should allow time for her to explore her feelings and then to make her own decision.

An alternative to abortion is, of course, to have the baby but then have it *adopted*. For those who want to hide the fact of their pregnancy and cannot afford to have the normal course of their life disrupted this is out of the question. Many women, too, are afraid that if they have the baby they will become too attached to it and at the last minute refuse to let it be adopted. They may well be right, for to part with the baby she has carried inside her for nine months and laboured to produce is a terrible wrench, even if she has as little as possible to do with the infant after the birth. However, for a minority who want the foetus to grow into a baby and could not bear an abortion but see no prospect of raising the child themselves, adoption is the answer.

With the greater availability of abortion, though, babies to adopt have become ever more scarce, and this is a poignant problem for those who are infertile. It is particulary galling, too, for women admitted to hospital for investigation of their *infertility* to find that so many others are in for abortion. A discussion of the physical causes of infertility, in either partner, is beyond the scope of this book, but it is worth mentioning the importance sometimes of psychological problems and faults of technique. Obviously conception cannot take place unless the sperm reaches the ovum in the womb, so if the man cannot get a stiff enough erection to penetrate his woman, or if he ejaculates very quickly, before he is properly inside her, or if she is too tense and tight to admit him properly, then conception cannot take place. If the position adopted for intercourse does not allow very full penetration then fertilization is the less likely. Psychological conflicts may affect the production of ova by the woman, may cause spasm of the tubes by which they reach the womb, may render the secretions at the neck of the womb less hospitable to sperm or may cause the vagina to expel the sperm containing fluid more rapidly after intercourse. And the disappointment and sense of failure or even shame after prolonged infertility may lead to avoidance of intercourse.

All these problems may well be helped by psychosexual counselling. The importance of anxiety and its relief is well demonstrated by the frequency with which an infertile couple, having at last managed to adopt a child, go on to produce one of their own very soon afterwards.

4

'I'm Pregnant!'

As a psychiatrist it interests me that women are rather more liable to suffer from mental disorder than men. This is partly because they live on average five years longer, and in old age the chances of developing a mental illness are much higher than in earlier life. But if we compare the sexes between the ages of fifteen and forty-five—a woman's childbearing years—we find that the risk to the female of developing psychological and emotional illness is significantly greater than to the male, and that this difference is more marked during this period of their lives than at any other.

The time when a woman is most at risk is during the three months after having a baby (see Chapter 11). However, during the nine months of pregnancy she seems almost protected from psychiatric disorder, or at least, from seeing a psychiatrist! Except, occasionally, for abortion counselling, psychiatrists see pregnant women remarkably rarely.

Does this mean, then, that pregnancy is a time of emotional stability and calm, unruffled bliss? Hardly! We all know from our personal experience that pregnant women tend to be moody, whimsical and to worry a lot. And, research confirms that pregnancy is associated with higher levels of anxiety than at other times.

While it is true that serious mental illness is very rare in pregnancy (for instance, admissions to psychiatric wards at this time are exceedingly unusual) milder emotional disturbance is very common. And the commonest of all is *anxiety*.

Often the first concern is to confirm the pregnancy. The

presence of a special hormone from the lining of the womb (chorionic gonadotrophin) in the urine can be detected from six weeks after conception. A positive test means that pregnancy is virtually certain. A negative result is less definite, and may turn positive a week or so later, after a good deal of nail-biting if the pregnancy is very much wanted—or feared!

The focus of the anxiety seems to move as the pregnancy progresses. In the first three months the main concern is, 'I'm pregnant!' In the second, the preoccupying question is, 'Will it be all right?' While in the last three months this partly gives way to 'How much longer will it last?'

Some 'I'm pregnant' worries have already been mentioned in Chapter 1. The change in role to becoming a mother, for the first time or again, arouses many fears almost from the moment that conception is recognized. The phrase 'falling for a baby' is eloquent. It suggests an accident rather than an intention (we don't willingly fall), a trap or pitfall laid by Fate rather than a desired goal. Unless menstruation is very irregular the first missed period is a strong indication of probable pregnancy, so the first indication is quite sudden—one day it seems that a woman is not pregnant, and a couple of days later she very probably is. It is almost as if pregnancy is the price to be paid for an active sex life—if she is unlucky she 'falls'. And the sudden change demands considerable adjustment.

For a woman who has never been pregnant before it might be expected that the 'fall' would be especially alarming. Fact and fantasy will cause her apprehension. In *fact*, life is going to change for her a lot. She is going to be tied and limited by a great responsibility. She will undergo a major physiological experience, involving discomfort, some pain and a small risk to her life. The attitudes of those near and dear to her will change somewhat, partly because she will have become a mother, and partly because of the baby she will produce. Simply because of her pregnancy she will have a lot to do with doctors, midwives, health visitors and other pregnant women who are also 'in the club' (another evocative phrase!). Money is likely to be a bit tighter, and she may well be faced with the problem of finding extra accommodation for the new arrival. She faces a unique challenge for which nothing yet in her life has wholly prepared her.

To this challenge she may rise, finding her personality enriched, gaining new strength and stability and taking a joy in her baby, watching him grow, sharing his discovery of the world, shaping his development and exploring the complexities of their relationship with love and fascination. At the other extreme, however, she may feel that her life is blighted and burdened and that her baby is a demanding drag.

Her *fantasies* are a blend of wishful thinking and fear of the unknown, both largely based upon smatterings of information, flights of imagination and suppressed dreads and longings since childhood. She may have a dream-like image of mother and baby, herself radiant and serene, her child smiling and beautiful, as docile and biddable as a doll with whom she used to play, the whole scene as romantic and unreal as a television commercial for toilet soap. Such escapism is partly nostalgia for a past that never was, partly a sweet but vain hope for a future which will redeem past failures and unhappiness by being more idyllic than human relationships are ever likely to be. But these glorious Technicolored daydreams are one of the pleasures of the early weeks of a first pregnancy, and do no harm provided they are not taken too seriously.

Frightening fantasies are partly derived from guilt over childhood conflicts and partly from the buried folklore which the business of childbirth seems inevitably to attract. Freud aroused a lot of hostility in his day by his concept of infantile sexuality. In Vienna at the turn of the century the idea that innocent children could have sexual feelings was extremely distasteful, and even in these enlightened or more sophisticated and permissive times there are many who find the notion disturbing. Freud would say this was because we don't wish to be made aware of what we ourselves felt as children; we don't want our deepest fears and most shameful secrets brought to light. However, little boys can have and enjoy an erection from an early age, and little girls may discover the pleasures of masturbation in infancy. Of course, they do not seek sexual intercourse, and are too young fully to comprehend the facts of life, but sexual curiosity and stimulation are an important part of the childhood play which prepares us for equivalent activities in adult life.

It is undoubtedly true that interest in the difference between the organs of the two sexes is intense. According to Freud the penis is regarded as a prize possession, and the fact that not all children have one causes alarm and envy. Perhaps the nursery chant, 'What are little girls made of? Sugar and spice and all things nice. What are little boys made of? Slugs and snails and puppy dogs' tails!' is based upon such envy. The less obtrusive delights of the vagina and the knowledge that this is the route to the girl's trump card, her ability to have a baby, are hardly known to young children, while the little boy's 'puppy dog's tail' is there for all to see (or, anyway, those in the bathroom, or joining the game of doctors and nurses). Freud's suggestion was that little girls may think that they've lost a penis, and little boys that they could! This is the basis of the 'castration complex' which relates infantile sexuality to aggression towards the parents, jealousy, guilt and the fear of punishment. So a little girl might fear she had already been damaged by the loss of a penis for rivalry with her mother for the exclusive love of her father, while a little boy might be so afraid of losing his penis for the crime of rivalry with his father for his mother ('the Oedipus complex'), that he might fail to develop adult sexuality and be impotent as a man, or fixated on a form of infantile sexuality such as fetishism, exhibitionsim or spanking.

Many psychoanalysts today think that Freud had overstressed the importance of the castration complex in adult life, but this and other repressed fears very probably account for some of the deepest anxieties of pregnancy. I will have more to say about these in the next chapter.

Folklore is an expression of superstition or the 'magical' thinking which is characteristic of childhood. Fairy stories, with princes, princesses, seventh sons, giants, dragons and witches who cast evil spells, are the very stuff of children's thoughts, in which to wish something is to try to make it happen and if the wish is a forbidden one, to invite retribution. It is magical thinking which gives such force to the feelings of childhood. The notion that, for example, seeing a deformed or blemished person can deform or birthmark the baby in the womb is likewise magical thinking, a carry-over from childhood. Women have built up a mystique of folklore about childbirth compounded of shared unconscious fears and fancies, a desire to support each other and a certain mischievous desire to put the wind up each other too. (Some old wives' tales might well be called 'old bitch's tales!')

Big as the change from having no baby at all to having the first may be, many women find that 'falling' for the second, third or a later baby is quite as challenging. Coping with two or more children is far more complicated than just coping with one, comparisons and competition and fairness have to be reckoned with, as well as all the extra work. So, whether it is the first baby or the fifth, pregnancy is likely to release a good deal of anxiety.

One of the earliest bodily changes the pregnant woman notices is in her breasts. They become fuller, so that the flat chested develop quite a full bust, while the already well endowed become quite voluptuous. The nipples enlarge and become extra sensitive, while the circles of skin surrounding them darken and stay dark for the rest of her life. Depending on how free she feels with her sexuality and her body, she may feel proud or ashamed of these changes, for several weeks the only consistent outward sign of her pregnancy, but her man is likely to appreciate them! The enlargement of the breasts is necessary for the eventual successful breast feeding of the baby, but because they are objects of sexual attraction and the nipples are erotically sensitive, the practical value of the changes can be obscured by the sexual implications

What about *sexual relations* during pregnancy? This is a frequent cause of worry. Should a woman want to make love when she's pregnant? Can it harm the baby? Will her partner want her still, especially when she appears heavy and swollen, or will he look elsewhere if they don't make love? The answers to all these questions, as to almost all the anxieties of pregnancy, are reassuring. It is perfectly normal for a woman to want sexual relations at this time. True, some find that they are less interested when pregnant, but others feel sexier than ever. Most men find their pregnant partners extremely attractive, and feel proud of and protective towards them. The extreme closeness of making love is exactly what the couple need to support each other and reaffirm the togetherness which gave rise to the pregnancy. The tiny foetus is well fixed to the wall of the womb and unlikely to be dislodged by this more than any other vigorous activity. However, where there have been several miscarriages the woman may be advised to lead as sedate a life as possible, and the couple may well decide that this means foregoing sexual intercourse for the first half of the pregnancy (though of course there are other ways of giving each other sexual satisfaction). Once the foetus has grown big enough to show, it is well insulated by the wall of the abdomen and the womb and the bag of (amniotic) fluid in which it lies, and won't be bruised. In the last weeks many women feel too tired (and fed up!) to want sex, and anyway by this time the size of the baby may make the traditional missionary position for sexual intercourse inconvenient, though a pillow or two beneath the woman's hips may make things a lot easier. However, for the eager and the enterprising it can be fun finding out other positions; where there's a will, there's certainly a way!

Are husbands unfaithful? Yes, sometimes. So, sometimes are wives. But most couples are faithful to each other, and husbands are far less likely to turn to other women when their wives are pregnant, however moody or exasperating they may be, than at a later, staler stage of the marriage.

One of the earliest symptoms of pregnancy is *nausea* or *vomiting*, especially in the mornings. This is quite normal, and a common side effect of pregnancy. Unlike the enlargement of the breasts, it is hard to see what useful purpose it serves. It probably results from the hormone changes of pregnancy, about which I shall have more to say later. It is very much associated with early pregnancy, and does not usually continue beyond the fourth month. There is little evidence to support the view that vomiting is a physical sign of psychological rejection of the pregnancy, an unconscious attempt, as it were, to 'sick up' the baby. However, there is a very serious form of excessive vomiting in pregnancy called hyperemesis gravidarum, and here psychological factors do seem to be important. The woman with hyperemesis is not only sick in the mornings, but all day, every day. She loses weight, becomes dehydrated, the balance of electrolytes in her body fluids is disturbed, and she is so ill that she must come into hospital or die. In hospital all is quickly put right by giving the necessary replacement fluid solutions into her veins and strangely very often while she is in hospital the vomiting stops. It seems then that the environment has a big effect on the vomiting.

Normal pregnancy vomiting is not at all dangerous and no cause for anxiety, but it is uncomfortable and a considerable nuisance, and certainly brings home the snags of being pregnant!

In the 1930s and '40s, films were far less outspoken than today when every other word of dialogue seems to have four letters. Instead of boldly stating, 'I'm pregnant' the heroine would faint, knit tiny garments or announce a sudden *craving* for raspberries, or pickled walnuts—whereupon the hero would get into a great state, and make her lie down and have to lie down himself. Typically, the craving would be for something tangy, for which she hadn't usually a taste, and which was not readily available. Are such cravings truly part of the process of pregnancy, or are they just folklore? Professor Trethowan of Birmingham University has reviewed the subject extensively, and finds that cravings, typically in early pregnancy, are a reality. One to two thirds of women, regardless of race or place, experience cravings or *aversions* to foods (or drinks) they normally like, or both. Sweet, salty, sour or savoury foods are preferred, especially those with a hard, crisp texture, such as an apple. A very small percentage of pregnant women crave substances normally regarded as inedible, such as coal, soap, toothpaste and mothballs!

Various explanations have been given for these cravings and aversions, none altogether satisfactory. Folklore and *superstition* may contribute, and a woman may feel that it is 'the thing' to crave if she is properly pregnant. In some primitive cultures there are beliefs that to eat this, or not to eat that, will either do good or harm, but that is not quite the same as having a craving. *Psychoanalysts* point out that to eat fruit, one of the commonest cravings, could be a magical way of taking in fruitfulness, and thus causing the pregnancy to prosper. It has been claimed that a *lack of necessary minerals* in the normal diet could partly account for some of the more bizarre cravings. Interestingly, studies of *taste threshhold* in pregnancy (though why would anybody think to study that?!) have show that the taste is somewhat blunted but returns to normal within hours of giving birth. So the craving for tangy, crunchy foods could well be because the ordinary diet tastes so bland. It is not impossible that a woman may occasionally use her craving, especially for some exotic or out of season food, somewhat whimsically, to test her power and see to what lengths her man will go for her. In other words she wants to be spoilt—and why not?

Occasionally through their cravings, but more often for other reasons, some women start to *overeat* in pregnancy, and end up overweight. With the baby growing rapidly in the womb some extra food is required, but appetite can easily exceed the need. Also it is possible that some foods are differently absorbed from the intestines during pregnancy, so that the same amount of food may be more fattening than usual. Not a few women have a tendency to stuff themselves when they feel worried or miserable, and of course anxiety and depression are commonly prominent in early pregnancy. They make up for feeling bad by putting good things inside them, they fill the 'aching void' with food, or they distract themselves from their unhappiness with a tasty morsel or three. Then they feel miserable about becoming fat, eat some more for comfort and a vicious circle begins.It is dangerous to be fat at any time, and especially during pregnancy when certain serious complications (such as toxaemia and high blood pressure) are more likely to develop in those who are overweight. An important part of antenatal care is to advise mothers-to-be on diet, what to eat and what to avoid (especially carbohydrates such as bread, potatoes, biscuits, pastries, cakes, sugar, jam, sweets and chocolates). A woman should not gain more than two stone (or fourteen kilograms) at the most in pregnancy.

Other physical accompaniments of pregnancy which

may be irksome are *frequency of urination*, constipation, low backache and fatigue.

The growing womb presses on the bladder which therefore feels full sooner than usual; any constipation will aggravate the problem of having to keep passing water. The kidneys are less able to produce a concentrated urine at night, so the pregnant woman must get up more often to pass water. Anxiety, which increases the tone of the bladder's muscular wall, makes matters worse. *Constipation* may be caused by changes in the absorption of food (already mentioned) leaving less roughage, and the muscles of the pelvic floor and of the bowel itself becoming lax in pregnancy. Antenatal exercises to strengthen these muscles and gain more conscious control over them are not only useful for overcoming constipation but also good practice for bearing down during labour. (They can also be used most effectively and enjoyably in sexual intercourse!)

As the womb grows it tilts forward and the centre of gravity of the mother moves forward with it. This can contribute to *backache*, as the lower part of the spine curves back to an unusual degree to accommodate the altered load. If the mother is depressed or demoralized the pain will feel worse to her. If she has put on extra weight, the strain of her back will be increased. Such postural backache can be eased by exercises and footwear to throw the weight back on the heels, about which the physiotherapist at the antenatal clinic or antenatal classes will advise.

The rate of metabolism, the process whereby we break down foodstuffs to give us energy for living, is increased in pregnancy, and this is one reason for *tiredness* at the end of the day. Also pregnant women easily become anaemic, the chief symptom of which is fatigue. They then need iron tablets as well as a good diet. Progesterone, one of the hormones produced in abundance during pregnancy (see below), has a sedative effect. Worry is wearying. Sleeplessness obviously aggravates the problem.

During the fortnight after the start of a period the ovaries secrete into the blood stream moderate quantities of a *hormone*, oestrogen, which causes the lining of the womb to enlarge, ready to receive the foetus if fertilization should take place. Once the ovum or egg has been produced the ovary also secretes another hormone, progesterone. If fertilization does not take place, the ovary stops secreting so much of the two hormones, which reach their lowest levels just before the next period. If the ovum is fertilized, however, it is implanted in the lining of the womb and the ovary goes on secreting oestrogen and progesterone in larger and larger quantities. The foetus receives its nourishment from the mother via the placenta or afterbirth, which forms at the place where it is fixed to the wall of the womb, and the placenta, too, secretes the two hormones (among others). As pregnancy progresses the production of the hormones is even higher, till just before delivery oestrogens are produced at ten times and progesterones at twenty-five times the maximum quantities during the normal menstrual cycle.

There can be little doubt that many women's emotions are considerably affected by the levels of the two hormones, and perhaps by the proportion of one to the other, though just how or why is less clear. Almost every other woman (anyway of my acquaintance!) seems to suffer from the pre-menstrual tension syndrome and is tense, irritable, depressed or bloated just before a period. The contraceptive pill is made up of oestrogen and/or progestogens, and appears to upset some women emotionally as well as physically. It would be surprising, then, if the major hormone changes during pregnancy were not accompanied by emotional changes in many women. To put it another way, the emotional vagaries of pregnant women are likely to be in part attributable to those hormone changes. *Depression*, in particular, which is almost as common as anxiety in early pregnancy, even when the pregnancy is evidently wanted, may sometimes be accounted for thus. Sudden despondency and tearfulness or irritability, lasting a few hours, all day, several days, or even two to three weeks, for the most trivial reason or none at all, causes the pregnant woman much distress, and her spouse and family hardly less. I've had requests for abortion where this depression has been so persistent in early pregnancy that the woman could not bear the thought of its continuance for another six or seven months, even though she really wanted the baby. Fortunately it has always cleared up before such drastic action had had to be taken

Having stated my belief that hormones are responsible for some emotional disturbances, I have to admit my reservations. The fact that some women get depressed, some broody and some are not affected at all might be explained by their different personalities and susceptibilities (though I don't think it has been shown that, for example, those who suffer pre-menstrual depression are likely to experience similar symptoms in pregnancy). However it is hard to see why, if the increase in oestrogen and/or progesterone in early pregnancy causes a woman to be depressed, the further increase as pregnancy continues does not necessarily cause her to be more depressed.

Having referred to Freud a few times already, I will now just mention his one-time disciple, Jung, in order to introduce the subject of *introversion* during pregnancy. Jung coined the words 'introvert' and 'extrovert' to describe personalities who live their lives, respectively, predominantly in an inner world of thoughts, feelings, fantasies and self-examination or in the outer world of actions and relationships, needing other people and making things happen. Women, especially those who get anxious readily, tend to become more introverted from the third month of pregnancy onwards. This is partly the action of the hormone progesterone, partly preoccupation with the growing foetus, which is a very important other being, yet at this stage still part of the self. The main manifestation of this introversion is the state of *broodiness* in which the pregnant woman is slow, passive, letting others bustle while she sits, and day-dreams of her baby. We all get a bit broody sometimes when we see babies or even young animals suckled, cuddled or stroked, and a pleasant, warm, scalp tingling experience it is. Women who like being broody when pregnant describe feeling like a contented cow, chewing the cud! However, naturally extrovert women who like to be up and doing find the broodiness vexatious, and resent being taken over by the pregnancy this way, feeling trapped by their biology in a sluggish, slow-witted, swollen body. Women who enjoy their broodiness are likely to enjoy breast-feeding, which induces a very similar state.

Towards the end of the first three months, most women are likely to pay their first visit to the *antenatal clinic* and, especially if they are pregnant for the first time, this is likely to arouse a good deal of anxiety. For the reasons I have set down in Chapter 7, in most developed countries the vast majority of confinements are in hospital. General practitioners give a good deal of antenatal care in their surgeries, and often have the use of some beds in the hospital's obstetric unit, so their patients are in at least one familiar pair of hands. But most women will be booked for delivery under the care of an obstetrician whom, if they have never before been pregnant, they are unlikely to have met before.

Hospital is a daunting place to those who are not familiar with it. The administrative arrangements often seem complicated and impersonal. Staff seem busy, rushed and preoccupied with more important matters. White coats and uniforms are somewhat intimidating. Who's who, and what do they do, and what do you call them can be difficult questions for the uninitiated. In the United Kingdom many hospitals are still Poor Law institutions modernized here and there with varying success, but grim, shabby and rambling. Even the impressive new hospitals and wings may seem rather clinical for comfort. Long corridors, strange sounds and smells, ambulances, stretchers and wheelchairs all, rightly, give the impression of an institution dealing with the sick. But, is pregnancy a sickness?

In Victorian days it was regarded as such, with some justification in view of the high maternal mortality in those days. Thanks, however, to the development of modern antenatal care and to the availability of antibiotics to combat the infections which so often used to prove fatal, pregnancy and childbirth are now as normal and natural and healthy as making love. True, it is slightly more hazardous, still, to life and health to have a baby than not to do so, but for the great majority of women the experience is safe and on the whole happy.

Although the antenatal clinic may seem a little forbidding and clinical to the newcomer, the staff are well aware that their patients are not patients, but healthy women whom they intend to keep healthy. Most medical students thoroughly enjoy working in obstetrics as it is so nice to deal with people who are well for a change!

The basic staff are doctors, midwives and health visitors. Leading the medical team is the *obstetrician*, who qualifies as a doctor and a surgeon before specializing in this field. Assisting him or her are junior doctors in training, G.P. assistants and, often, medical students. Most *students* are keen to learn, well supervised and take a keen personal interest in any women they deliver.

The *midwives* are trained nurses with extra training and experience in the care of women before, during and after childbirth. They have taken the place of the experienced mothers and grandmothers who attended the confinement in former times (and still do in less developed societies) and of the dreadful, drunken Mrs Gamps of a hundred years ago.

The *health visitor* is a nurse who has undergone further training in domestic and community health. She has special knowlege of child development and the mother–child relationship, and takes a particular interest in the social circumstances.

Other specialist staff who are available at or via the antenatal clinic are the dietician, physiotherapist, social worker, dentist and occasionally the psychiatrist!

At the first visit to the clinic a fairly full history is taken of past pregnancies as well as the present one, past illnesses and the present circumstances. A medical examination will include taking the blood pressure; anxiety always pushes this up, so it may well be taken again when the woman is a little more relaxed. At this visit or a later one there will be an internal (vaginal) examination which many women dread, fearing embarrassment far more than discomfort. The privacy of this part of themselves is very understandable and to be respected—what the doctor does would be indecent assault in another context!—but the examination enables him to find out the state and size of the womb and the shape and dimensions of the pelvis. The size of the womb may be a better indication than dates of the duration of the pregnancy. Many women are very hazy indeed about the timing of the last monthly period (L.M.P.) and it is obviously necessary to know when the baby is to be expected, the estimated date of delivery (or E.D.D.). A woman's hips are wider than a man's (had you noticed?), wide enough indeed for the head of a newborn baby to pass from the upper to the lower abdomen through the bony ring of pelvis and thus to be pushed out into the world altogether. The width of the hips alone is an unreliable indication of the width of this channel but those whose hips are narrow and boyish may be in difficulties. The vaginal examination tells how roomy the pelvis is, and whether there is any likelihood that the baby's head may not easily be pushed through. The pregnant mother is weighed and samples are taken of her blood and her urine. Blood tests include grouping, in case a transfusion should ever be needed, and examinations for anaemia and venereal disease. The urine is tested for sugar, which indicates diabetes, and protein which might suggest an infection of the bladder or kidneys or, at a later stage, toxaemia. Routine X-rays are avoided because of the slight risk of harming the reproductive organs of the developing foetus.

At the antenatal clinic the mother-to-be meets other mothers-to-be. I'll have more to say about them in Chapter 6. For the first seven months of pregnancy a monthly attendance usually suffices, but there are two visits in the eighth month and one every week in the last. So the support and supervision intensify as (E.D.) D-day approaches!

5

'Will It Be All Right?'

After the alarm and astonishment, the excitement and dismay, the challenge and bewilderment of early pregnancy, the second three months are a period of relative calm. I say relative, because apprehension and anticipation are still at a high pitch; while there is a major happening at about four and a half months' pregnant—*quickening*. The mother can actually feel her baby stirring inside her, and pushing against the wall of the womb, announcing in a way which cannot be denied, 'I'm here'.

Until this moment it is still possible for the mother only half to believe in her pregnancy, to disregard the absent periods, her fuller figure, the morning sickness and think of the foetus as no more than a collection of cells, or even a mere idea which may yet be dispelled, but with quickening the reality of the baby's existence can no longer be resisted.

The movements resolve much of the early ambivalence of pregnancy. Few mothers, though they may have resented the great changes in their life that pregnancy brings, do not feel strongly that they want the baby once it has made its presence felt.

When you come to think of it (or at least, when I do) the idea of a baby growing inside the mother is pretty remarkable. Some people find it quite hard to believe in their own reality. The chaplain in Christopher Fry's delicious comedy, *The Lady's Not for Burning*, says, 'When I think of myself I can scarcely believe my senses. But there it is, all my friends tell me I exist and by an act of faith I have come to believe them.'

Though I was brought up as a Christian I have always found the idea of the Trinity hard to grasp, and for anyone at all uncertain of her own identity, the duality of the two-in-one of pregnancy must be somewhat perplexing. Small wonder is it, then, that some mothers feel quite unreal at times during pregnancy, have difficulty in believing that the baby is really theirs and can't wholly accept what is happening to them. Other women may feel frankly disturbed by the thought that there is a creature growing inside them, feeding on them like a parasite. They may be angry, resentful and even frightened of this strange thing within them, which seems to stand for the bad part of themselves that they would like to disown. Such fantasies were given full scope in the book and film *Rosemary's Baby*, about a woman who gets impregnated by the devil.

However, for most women quickening brings a surge of *maternal feeling* which makes all the troubles of pregnancy up to that moment seem of small account. The foetus turns into a baby and becomes very precious. Now the relationship between mother and child really begins.

Self-love is often confused with selfishness, and deplored. In fact it is essential to have respect and regard for oneself, to find oneself worthy of love, in order to feel inner security and to love others freely. Those who feel bad and unlovable either shun loving relationships or exploit them, anxiously seeking the reassurance that they are good after all, but unable to accept it.

The woman secure in self-love finds with quickening an extra part of herself to love—her baby. Very probably the special qualities of mother love, the tenderness, joy, unselfishness and tolerance, derive from this delighted and legitimate love of the self.

It is reassuring to know that the baby is alive in there, and kicking, but the middle months of pregnancy are to some extent overshadowed by the biggest anxiety of all: '*Will it be all right?*' This fear is there almost as soon as the awareness of pregnancy, but as the early anxieties fade this one comes to predominate. In my London Hospital survey the other main worry at this time was about delivery. I'll be discussing this at length later in this chapter, but I found an interesting difference between anxiety about the baby and anxieties about the birth. Anxiety about the baby seems to be more fundamental, and closely correlated with the level of general anxiety and depression. And two-thirds of the women in my survey were worrying about their babies a lot.

How justified, in reality, is this worry? The incidence of *congenital abnormalities* varies somewhat from country to country, and with the age of the mother, how many pregnancies she's had already, and her socio-economic class, but in this country about 2 per cent of babies are born with some abnormality. Still-births and deaths in the first week after birth (just under 2 per cent) and premature births (5·9 per cent), should perhaps be added to this, bringing the risk up to 10 per cent. If the 10 per cent who miscarry are added (and among the foetuses lost this way, many are grossly abnormal) the total risk that the pregnancy will not end in the birth of a live and wholly normal baby is about 1 in 5.

Some abnormalities are so severe that although born alive, the baby is bound to die in a few days. Among the serious disorders despite which the baby may survive are abnormalities of the heart and great blood vessels, spina bifida and mongolism (Down's Syndrome). On the whole disorders which cause physical deformity or mental subnormality are those most dreaded. (See also Chapter 12.)

Great publicity has been given to two causes of damage to the developing foetus, infections and drugs. The publicity has certainly increased general awareness of these risks and has probably heightened maternal anxiety. The main *infection* is, of course, the otherwise harmless German measles (rubella), which is very liable to injure the foetus, and the development of the heart and blood vessels in particular, at about the eighth week of pregnancy, and to cause deafness over a longer period. For this reason many parents used to try to see that their daughters caught rubella while they were young, but vaccination is now available to schoolgirls and susceptible women. If a woman has caught the disease in early pregnancy the risk of damage to her foetus is such that abortion is justified under the laws of many countries. This doesn't mean, though, that every cough or cold which a pregnant woman may suffer will endanger her baby!

Drugs have been notorious bogies ever since the discovery that thalidomide, a very useful and safe sleeping tablet, stopped the development of the foetal limbs, so that the babies were born with stumps instead of arms and legs. Other, less familiar drugs have been shown to affect the baby at different times and in different ways during pregnancy, but the vast majority of drugs commonly in use today have not been shown to harm the foetus at all. There's always a problem with new drugs, which are tested on animals before being given to people. It cannot confidently be assumed that what is safe for animals is safe for people.

Women have become nervous about taking any drugs in pregnancy, and many doctors have become nervous about prescribing them. It is wise to avoid the use of any drug unless there are very definite reasons for giving it. However it seems to me over-cautious to withhold a tranquillizer or an anti-depressive from a woman who is particularly anxious or depressed in pregnancy if it is likely to ease her distress at no known risk to her baby.

It is ironical, though very human, that a woman who may be very anxious in case she took an aspirin before she knew she had conceived continues to smoke throughout her pregnancy! Although *smoking* is unlikely to cause major abnormality it is certainly associated with smaller babies, slower to develop both physically and intellectually, than those of non-smokers. If the mother is a smoker she may well react to the tensions of pregnancy by smoking more. However, this is clearly a particularly good time to give up smoking altogether. That is more easily said than done, Heaven knows, but strong motivation and a good present reason help enormously.

There is evidence that radiation can damage the reproductive organs of the foetus, and increase the likelihood that the future adult will conceive abnormal children. For this reason X-rays are avoided, where possible, not only in women known to be pregnant, but also in the last half of the time between periods just in case they might be.

Infections in early pregnancy and the effects of drugs account for about 1 in 50 of abnormal babies. The vast majority are due to faults in *genes*, carried in the chromosomes of the germ cells, or sometimes in the chromosomes themselves, so that from the moment of conception the abnormality is inevitable. Changes in the chromosomes (mutations) are likely to occur in the germ cells of older women, which is why they are more likely to give birth to mongols. Where the parents are closely related (first cousins for example) the chance of abnormality in their offspring is much increased. But otherwise the bearing of an abnormal baby is simply a matter of bad luck.

From all the foregoing it is clear that the risk that the baby will not be all right is not negligible. The anguish of giving birth to a seriously handicapped child and having it die, or rejecting it or accepting the burden of its care, cannot be denied. Yet do these realities sufficiently account for the deep and widespread fear of such a calamity? I doubt it.

This particular fear is a conscious expression of the pregnant woman's fundamental *unconscious dread*, that of being punished, blighted for her sins of rivalry with, resentment of, ill-wishing and trying to oust her mother. Infantile fantasies of pregnancy by ingestion may lead to the idea of the foetus as bad food, curdled milk, which will make the woman suffer for what the child devoured with such greedy aggression. On the other hand, the guilty woman may fear that her badness will taint the foetus, which will then grow into a monster which, being born, will proclaim her monstrous wickedness to the world. Or, in fantasy, the vengeful mother may have cursed her rebellious daughter's womb so that she cannot bear normal children herself. The baby may be thought of as stolen from the mother and inevitably to be taken back.

It has been suggested that the process of repression, whereby such alarming memories of the conflicts of childhood are kept from our consciousness, is relaxed somewhat during pregnancy. Thus the pregnant woman is unusually aware of ideas and feelings which are normally unconscious and when she broods, panics, is half asleep or in the company of other pregnant women these strange, disturbing thoughts and fantasies are very near to consciousness.

One advantage of this availability of material normally locked away is that it may be re-examined. In psychoanalysis the patient is helped day by day over several years to nibble away at the edges of the unconscious, guided by dreams and the chain of thoughts which he can allow into his conscious mind while lying on the analyst's couch. Gradually he learns about the fears and strivings which have determined so much of his adult behaviour and pondering them now as a thoughtful adult, no longer a frightened child, he can sort out fact from fiction, see things in proportion and gain self-knowledge and maturity. The pregnant woman can do something of the same sort, much more quickly and even without the guidance of an analyst. Quite a lot of women 'grow up' in the course of a pregnancy. It is not so much the responsibility of motherhood which makes them more *mature*, but the working through of old conflicts with the unusual insight of pregnancy.

Thus pregnancy may provide a chance to find new solutions to old, unsolved problems.

Not every woman of course is able to take this opportunity. Many are essentially unchanged and some are so frightened by this glimpse of their inner selves that they become more nervous and inhibited than they were before. Probably, however, during pregnancy the influence of an informed and understanding other person can help a woman to recognize, accept and use her new feelings about herself, rather than be 'scared off' them. For this reason doctors and midwives can be extra helpful to the women in their care if they have the will and find the time to respond to their feelings, as well as their physical progress through pregnancy. Within a few weeks of the baby's birth the barriers to the unconscious are back again, and the opportunity has been lost.

As noted in the previous chapter the return to near consciousness of so many childhood memories brings a return to the *magical thinking* of childhood, so that supersititions, obsessions and rituals are rife in pregnancy. Some women feel most secure when hedged about by prohibitions. They take the advice of the antenatal clinic as gospel truth, and dare not deviate in the least from their instructions. They are likely to find quite a few extra rules and regulations to follow slavishly too. This obsessional regard for order seeks to control an uncertain and confused, even chaotic, situation and to bow to the demands of a strict and dominating conscience. The careful observation of rules, though sensible up to a point, is basically the same sort of behaviour as the child's avoidance of lines on the pavement to avoid bad luck in general or a particular misfortune.

Ideally this is a time at which *mother and daughter* should draw especially close (see Chapter 2). Nothing can be more reassuring to the pregnant woman than to have her mother's firm approval of her pregnancy. If her mother is clearly delighted at the thought of becoming a grandmother, and if her help is given freely, it is my impression that fears for the foetus are rarely severe. However, such happy reconciliations may not be possible. The mother may be dead, or live too far away, or dislike her son-in-law, or indeed disapprove of the pregnancy, feeling slighted or jealous, or that her daughter is too young to have a baby, cannot afford one or is spoiling her career. There may be a coolness between mother and daughter, based on old feelings of rivalry for the father or favouritism to a brother or sister, or the mother's inability to show or give affection, which cannot be thawed. The pregnant daughter may totally reject the model of mothering given by her mother, and want to raise her child so differently that she cannot seek her help. Guilt or resentment may be so strong that she cannot come close to her mother or forgive her. She is then, I believe, especially a prey to morbid fears.

If there are reasons to indicate that the foetus may be abnormal, or if the woman's fears are such that she is frantic for reassurance, it may be possible to find out whether there is a particular abnormality by performing blood tests and then, if the results are suggestive, drawing off some of the fluid from the sack in which the foetus lies before the pregnancy has gone too far to be terminated. By this procedure—*amniocentesis*—cells from the foetus may be examined for the abnormalities of chromosomes characteristic of mongolism, or for levels of a particular protein in the fluid which show that spina bifida is very likely. However amniocentesis is not altogether without risk—there is a possibility of causing a bleed from the afterbirth, or starting a premature labour—so its use has to be reserved for cases where it is really necessary to know what is going on. An extra piece of information which can be obtained, by the way, is the sex of the foetus. Cells from a female in the fluid stain differently from those of a male, so the mother has the advantage, such as it is, of knowing well in advance whether she is going to have a little boy or a little girl.

If there is to be a *miscarriage* (doctors use the phrase 'spontaneous abortion' but this may be confusing to the lay person) it is likely to have happened before the pregnancy is halfway through. For the woman who has almost decided that she wants the pregnancy terminated anyway it is something of a relief, absolving her of the responsibility of taking a decision, but for other mothers it is a deep disappointment. Not only is there depression over the loss of the pregnancy, a feeling of futility and waste, but also shame and guilt are not uncommon. There is a sense of failure of femininity, a fear that the genital apparatus is damaged or faulty, and a racking of the brains for whatever misdeed might have caused the loss of the pregnancy. 'Was it because I got so angry the other day, or we made love on Saturday night, or you took me to that horror film, or I forgot I was pregnant and did the spring cleaning? Was it because I wasn't altogether pleased after I'd missed the first period, and by the time I'd decided I wanted to be pregnant the damage was done?' The loss of the pregnancy brings right to the surface the fears, fantasies and magical thinking which have been discussed at some length in this chapter.

Those who have three or more miscarriages have been shown, like those who suffer from primary infertility or hyperemesis, to include more immature, dependent, obsessional and maritally dissatisfied women than those who have only one or two, and naturally it has been suggested that ambivalence about the pregnancy can render the hold of the foetus on the womb precarious. I see no reason for doubting that this is sometimes true, but there are undeniable physical factors in habitual miscarriages, and it is to be expected that a woman who badly wants a baby and keeps miscarrying is going to show signs of psychological stress and strain.

Women who have miscarried are likely to avoid sexual intercourse in the early months of pregnancy, and are probably well advised to do so for the first three months.

To mothers especially anxious about the welfare of the baby inside them it can be greatly reassuring to hear the beating of its tiny *heart*. This is possible from the twentieth week onwards. I remember as a medical student straining to hear something through a foetal stethoscope. Technical developments have been considerable since then, though, and it is now practicable to let the mother hear the heart-beat herself, or even to see it on a monitor screen.

The other main anxiety, or group of anxieties, in the middle period of pregnancy is the *labour* itself. Of course, this is a worry from the outset, especially to those who have never been pregnant before (and it worries quite a few women before they ever get to be pregnant) but, as the early anxieties about being pregnant at all recede, this one remains and becomes more prominent.

The main concern is the *pain* of childbirth—how bad will it be, and how well endured? Most women fear that the pain will be the worst they have ever suffered and, to be honest, for all the benefits of psychoprophylaxis, and 'natural' childbirth and with modern anaesthesia and analgesia, some of these women are not wrong. In the 'stiff upper lip' cultures, the fear of giving way noisily to the pain and disgracing herself by yelling the place down, is actually greater than the fear of the pain itself. Another anxiety is that the birth will *damage* the mother. How can the baby's head be pushed through a passage which seemed very adequately filled by a penis before pregnancy? How can it not split the womb, the skin or even its mother in two?

Well, this is one of nature's conjuring tricks, rather like the parlour trick of easing a coin through a slit in a piece of paper shorter than its diameter, though just as the paper sometimes tears, so there is sometimes a bit of splitting of the skin as the baby's head comes through. Quite often, in fact, the doctor or midwife anticipates this by making a cut which is stitched up afterwards. The womb has the capacity to dilate until the neck is wide enough for the baby to be pushed out (or else birth would hardly take place!) and never splits unless the powerful muscular wall has been weakened by, say, a previous Caesarian section, and only exceedingly rarely even then. And I've never heard of a woman splitting in two!

The thought of *losing control* is alarming to some women—of going berserk, making a mess, and being 'taken over' by the inevitable process of birth. A great advantage of the methods of 'natural' childbirth and psycho-prophylaxis, which can be taught in antenatal classes (see below) is that they increase a woman's control of and harmony with labour. But birth *can* be somewhat messy, and women often lose their inhibitions at the time and are more emotional and outspoken than usual—and who shall blame them? Anyway, what does it matter? Midwives are bound to see women undergoing the greatest transition of their lives and are hardly likely to be perturbed by yells, screams, oaths or a bit of soiling, so long as the baby is moving well on its way.

Another fear is that of *losing consciousness*, either because of fainting or anaesthesia. This is what many people fear most about an operation, though I suppose they'd be more afraid still if they thought of having surgery without being anaesthetized! All sorts of horrible things might be going on when one was unconscious—one might not even wake up! Actually women are very unlikely to faint during labour and as the importance of their being conscious, especially at the moment of birth, is given more and more recognition, anaesthesia is only used to the point of inducing complete oblivion where the treatment of complications makes it necessary. Anaesthetists are increasingly able to relieve pain without eliminating consciousness.

Complications, of course, are dreaded—getting stuck in labour and having to have forceps or a Caesarian section, bleeding, having a heart attack, damaging the baby, dying. All I will say about these at present is that the chance that a woman will die in childbirth is very low, of the order of one in more than 8,000 births. Yet a small proportion of women are so terrified of not surviving that they will not embark on a pregnancy at all, even though they would like to have a child. If, nevertheless, they do conceive, they can't imagine that they will end the pregnancy alive, and with a live baby. The fear quite blights their marital lives. The basis of this is usually a deep conviction that the penalty for presuming to usurp their mother's role must be death.

As most deliveries nowadays take place in hospital, there are anxieties associated with being *away from home*, in a strange place and in the hands of strangers. Some rather protected women have never been away from home before and are afraid of being homesick. Hospital, as has been remarked in the previous chapter, is a strange and bewildering place to the uninitiated and the thought of uniforms, transfusions, and emergencies may be pretty awesome. The staff are unknown, and might be belittling, impersonal or uncaring. The other women may be catty, embarrassing or tiresome. And there is often a fear of being alone, in a side ward or up a corridor, at a critical moment in the labour when all the staff are busy elsewhere. The more the mother-to-be learns what to expect in hospital at the antenatal clinic the better she gets to know the staff (especially the midwife who is likely to deliver her), the more hospitable hospital will seem, and if her husband is going to be present while she has the baby then she need not fear being alone. By now the pregnant woman should have been to the antenatal clinic more than once, and will be getting to know some of the other mothers attending with her. As they sit together in the waiting room or area, sometimes in a state of anonymous half undress which, however regrettable, tends to eliminate the differences of personality and social class which clothes suggest, there is usually time to talk. Information is exchanged, anxieties are shared, reassurance is offered, alarmist tales, perhaps, are spread, and an atmosphere of bawdy, down-to-earth, cheerful vulgarity prevails. I am told that the lowering of the barrier to the unconscious mind in pregnancy gives an unusually colourful, even lurid quality to these conversations—'The colonel's lady and Judy O'Grady', both now members of the 'club', let their hair down and talk of men, mothers, mothers-in-law, midwives, births and babies, sex and Caesarian sections, periods and pregnancy, children and the change. They share hopes, fears and feelings, reminisce, sometimes embellishing their memories more than a little, and speculate, letting their fantasies run away with them at times, at others taking sober thought for the future. The atmosphere is a bit rich, perhaps, but sustaining. All this I am told, but I am also told that the staff are rarely party to these discussions, so I don't quite know how the secret leaked out, except that staff not infrequently become or have been members of the 'club' themselves! Be that as it may, these informal get-togethers at the antenatal clinic are a form of unstructured *group therapy*, providing a great deal of mutual support.

A more organized and official form of group therapy is an occasional feature of *antenatal classes.* The group therapy is a very useful way of facing, exploring and coming to terms with feelings for those who are 'all in the same boat'! There is likely to be a therapist who may focus and direct the group's work, or make interpretations about what the group may be doing as a whole. However, most classes are more concerned with physiology than psychology and with teaching rather than interpretations. A great deal of valuable information is forthcoming about the process and effects of pregnancy, medical problems and complications, the development of the foetus, the stages of labour, the beginning of the relationship between mother and child, infant feeding, welfare and child care. Advice is available on what to wear in pregnancy, what to eat, how to exercise, and what to do and not to do. The best classes avoid or explain medical jargon, which can unnecessarily put the wind up women whose imagination is already heightened by pregnancy. In particular women are taught by the methods of '*natural*' *childbirth* or *psychoprophylaxis* how to relax and breathe during labour, how to use muscles of whose existence they were barely aware, so that they may work in harmony with the contractions of the womb to enjoy an efficient delivery. It is untrue to say that 'natural' childbirth eliminates pain, but it renders it quite tolerable and even pleasurable as an intrinsic part of pushing a baby out into the world.

The image of the tribal African woman in the bush who is working in the fields, goes into labour, has her baby behind a tree, goes back to the fields and returns to her village with the baby at the end of the day, is a most appealing one. But the risk of childbirth, to mother and baby, is far higher under such primitive circumstances than in a modern obstetric service. Natural childbirth, recognizing that fear and the preoccupation that the pain must be very severe actually make for a more painful and difficult labour, helps the pregnant woman to cope with the delivery as naturally and harmoniously as this fabled African woman in the bush, despite, even, the setting of a modern labour ward.

It is important that mothers-to-be appreciate that they are likely to experience some pain, or when they actually do so they may feel unduly alarmed. Over-enthusiastic promoters of 'natural' childbirth in the past have caused some women to feel embittered or ashamed when the labour turned out to hurt far more than they had expected—either the method was a confidence trick or they were not natural women. The point is that the pain is accepted as part of the joyful act of giving birth, and recognized as bearable, manageable and worthwhile so that the unique experience can be endured in full consciousness.

Women who are to be delivered in hospital need to know that there is going to be some high powered technology around. Otherwise the sight of inductions and monitoring may cause them to lose heart and feel that the business of childbirth is going to be beyond their own simple resources.

The *husband's presence* at the antenatal class is very desirable. There was for a long time a 'conspiracy of women' view of childbirth, which excluded the father after he had perpetrated the dark deed which started the pregnancy. Having had his selfish way his wife had to pay, and the mysterious travail of labour, the agony he had inflicted upon his wife, was not for him to know about until he was finally admitted to see her haggard, but smiling bravely, and the newborn baby in as neat a bundle as if the stork had brought it. It is only relatively recently that men were admitted to this secret rite even as obstetricians, while there is still considerable resistance to the idea of male midwives.

However, over the past fifteen years or so the father has been given more and more of a place, as it has been discovered how much he has to contribute. He can be a great support to his wife as he shares the experience of pregnancy with her. During labour, in particular, his company prevents loneliness, and his comfort, co-operation and encouragement can be a great help in coping with the womb's fierce contractions and in his wife's pushing efficiently when the time comes. He may have learnt the technique of natural childbirth or psychoprophylaxis with her and be an excellent coach when at last these techniques are to be used. Having participated in the delivery he is likely to feel fully involved, and gladly share the burdens of the trying postnatal period. There is evidence that where husbands attend antenatal classes with their wives the likelihood of emotional disturbances after the baby's birth is less, though it is possible that those husbands who are prepared to go to the classes are also those most likely to help as much as possible once the baby is born.

To conclude this chapter I should like to mention that during this middle period of pregnancy some women are blissfully *contented*—more so, perhaps, than at any previous time in their lives. This is a development of that broodiness mentioned in the last chapter. There is a dreamy, delighted anticipation of the joys of motherhood, without the harsh realities which qualify the rapture of the actual experience. The langourous sensuality of these months means that sex is sometimes enjoyed as never before. Consequently occasionally women find pregnancy so agreeable that they have no sooner delivered one child than they gladly fall for the next. It is not that they are particularly motherly; the large families, one child born barely a year after another, are somewhat neglected by their abstracted, yet again pregnant mother, and when she can conceive no more she wakes up, comes to, and finds she has so many children she doesn't know what to do!

While only a few women find pregnancy so addictive, this happy phase is a bonus for many. Not only do they feel good, but they look good. They ripen and bloom, the complexion clears, they glow and sparkle and look especially beautiful. Like many other men I feel that a woman is never more attractive than when happily pregnant.

6

'How Much Longer?'

The last three months of pregnancy is a time of growing physical discomfort, occasional complications, fairly frequent depression and almost universal impatience.

Those who have been working will usually stop at around the seventh month. They feel tired, heavy, ungainly and need more rest than is compatible with any but a very local and sedentary job. Also, a maternity allowance is payable in this and some other countries at this time. Feelings about this change, seen by some as a final capitulation to the demands of motherhood, are inevitably mixed. It may be a relief to concentrate solely on becoming a mother and, if the job was uninteresting, to give up what has become a chore and a drag. Even so, the companionship of workmates may be missed, and the first few days at home can be very lonely. To those who valued their work the final wrench may be painful and the loss of occupational role lower their self-esteem. Uncertainty about when it will be resumed, the discomfort of the pregnancy at this stage and a sense of greater dependency on the spouse all tend to stir up the negative feelings of early pregnancy.

However time is moving on towards the inevitable dénouement, and soon the labour and delivery are preoccupations which displace regrets over what has been relinquished. For many women, though, the time seems to crawl at a snail's pace. They feel fat and fed up, the estimated date of delivery seems a long way off, and they sincerely hope not to be a day overdue.

The abdominal swelling tends to be bigger in women who have already had a baby, whatever the size of the actual infant inside them, because the abdominal muscles are laxer after a first childbirth. But the woman who has never been pregnant before feels quite plump enough at this stage! In the last month of pregnancy, though, there should be a 'lightening' of her distension as the baby's head engages in the pelvic cavity, so that only its body remains in the abdomen. Engagement tends to occur a little later in those who have already had a baby. Engagement is a reassuring development; once the baby's head is in the pelvis all is set fair for the onset of labour.

By this time, especially if it is the summer, most women are bored with maternity clothing, and long to regain their figures and have access to their full wardrobe, and be in the fashion again. Their impatience, then, is partly a desire to be free of the discomforts of pregnancy, partly an eagerness to see their baby at last, and partly a very natural desire to be their normal selves again.

The physical discomfort of pregnancy certainly increases in these last three months. Vomiting is no longer a problem, as a rule, but there is *heartburn* instead. The pressure of the enlarged womb within the abdomen, and the relaxation of certain muscles during pregnancy as a result of the increased secretion of the hormone progesterone mean that the stomach contents are easily regurgitated up the gullet. This painful burning sensation behind the breastbone tends to be worse when the woman is lying down at night, and can interfere with her much needed sleep.

Another problem particularly likely to be troublesome at night is *cramps* in the legs. The cause of these is not really known. The cramps are sudden and painful, in the calves, and last about a minute or two. No treatment is consistently effective. Like heartburn, it is one of the small crosses which have to be borne in late pregnancy.

Varicose veins and *piles* are especially likely to occur at this time in those who are predisposed to get them anyway. The cause is probably a combination of the enlarged womb increasing the pressure in the abdominal cavity and a laxity of the walls of the veins. Piles are essentially varicose veins in the wall of the anus and are aggravated by constipation, straining to open the bowels and sitting too long on the lavatory. They may cause itching or burning, or spattering of blood when the bowels are opened which is alarming, but never serious. Varicose veins cause the legs to feel heavy and look unsightly. Piles are less trouble if constipation can be avoided, and varicose veins are eased by keeping the feet up as much as possible and wearing supportive stockings. Both these problems soon diminish after the baby's birth but will recur in subsequent pregnancies.

A *vaginal discharge* is not uncommon in pregnancy, and quite healthy unless heavy, itchy or especially smelly, in which case there may be infection which should be treated.

Infection of the kidneys and bladder occurs more easily in pregnancy than at other times. It increases the frequency of urination still further, and causes the urine to scald as it is passed. It is important to get treatment for this condition, which is otherwise associated with increased risk of high blood pressure at the end of pregnancy and a premature delivery.

Well before the onset of labour the *womb contracts* from time to time. The contractions cause some pain, going through to the small of the back, and can easily be felt by the husband as a tightening and hardening of the womb lasting for about ten to twenty seconds. Such 'Braxton Hicks' contractions become more frequent once the head is engaged. By now the *foetus* is quite lively. Temperamentally some seem more active than others, and at their most vigorous they can kick about quite remarkably, keeping the mother and even the father awake at night. Gerald Caplan quotes a rueful father, 'He's not born yet, and already the little b. . . . is trying to kick me out of bed!'

Fatigue increases towards the end of pregnancy, so that

many women find that they do not get enough sleep at night, but need to take a rest in the afternoon as well. Any desire for sex usually goes off at this time. Eager though most women are by now to get on with labour, as they lay their weary heads to the pillow it is often with the thought, 'let me sleep through tonight!'

A fairly common complication of the last months of pregnancy is the mysterious *toxaemia*. The name suggests a toxin or poison in the blood, which is misleading, for no such cause has been found, nor seems very likely. The main symptom is retention of fluid in the body. A little swelling of the ankles at the end of the day is normal at this time, but to wake with puffy eyelids, to find one's fingers swollen and the wedding ring too tight, to have swollen legs and ankles in the morning or early afternoon, and to gain a lot of extra weight in the last half of pregnancy (more than 0.5 kg or 1 lb a week) all indicate retention of fluid. The main signs of toxaemia, easily detectable by the doctor or nurse at the antenatal clinic, are a rise in blood pressure and the leakage of protein into the urine.

Toxaemia occurs in 8 per cent of first, and about 4 per cent of subsequent pregnancies. Untreated, it carries the risk of stillbirth, and a very dangerous (and fortunately now very rare) condition called eclampsia, the most striking symptom of which is fits. There is also a slight risk of continuing high blood pressure and of kidney disorders after the birth, though far more commonly the end of the pregnancy means the end of the toxaemia too.

The risk of toxaemia is one of the reasons why visits to the antenatal clinic are more frequent as pregnancy draws to its end. Another is to ensure that the baby is properly positioned for the delivery, with the head down and engaged in the pelvis. If the baby's head is up and its bottom down, however, there may be a breech delivery which is rather trickier than being born head first. To avoid this attempts are occasionally made to turn the baby round in the womb, so that its head is down, and then to push the head so that it engages in the pelvis. Once the head is engaged it is unlikely to be dislodged. Also during one of the final visits there will probably be another vaginal examination to ensure that there is no obstruction to the passage of the baby's head.

One of the anxieties in late pregnancy, especially in women who have never had a baby, is *when will labour start*, and *how to know* that it has started. I can sympathize with these worries, for although I am a doctor and more than once a father, I was never altogether sure that labour hadn't started a few days before it actually had.

'*False labour*' is frequently confusing—a series of womb contractions which start more strongly than they go on, and eventually die away, but not always before the mother finds herself in hospital, all ready to deliver, only to feel slightly foolish!

The *show* of a plug of blood-stained jelly from the mouth of the womb is a very good sign that labour is about to start, but easily overlooked. When the 'water break', i.e. the bag of amniotic fluid which bathes the baby bursts under the pressure of the contracting womb, labour proceeds apace, but this rarely happens at the beginning, but usually when labour is well under way.

The surest indication of labour is *repeated regular contraction of the womb*. The contractions, felt as a sort of cramp in the small of the back and the womb, associated with a tightening easily felt by a hand on the abdominal wall, at first last no more than twenty seconds and occur at about every twenty minutes. However, they become more frequent and last longer, till by the end of the first stage of labour they occur for one to one and a half minutes every three to four minutes.

Parents worry about whether labour will start *at an inconvenient time*. They needn't, because it nearly always does! Only induction can guarantee convenience. Otherwise the small hours and social engagements seem especially likely to be interrupted by the onset of labour.

Obstetricians learn to accept this with resignation—nights without sleep and a disrupted social life are especially their lot, though it's a nice job otherwise—and parents-to-be should try to do the same. Though some mothers may rather resent being taken over by the physiology of reproduction, the end of pregnancy really belongs to the baby. (Actually labour is just as likely to start at any hour in the 24 as at any other. As the majority of these fall outside 9 a.m. to 5 p.m., labour and childbirth are nearly always inconvenient.) A more important worry is whether they will get to hospital or call the midwife *too late*. Fantasies of having the baby in a train or a taxi, or at home without expert help, are alarming. Happily however such mishaps are extremely rare. There are hours between the onset of labour and a first delivery, plenty of time for getting to the right place or calling for the necessary assistance. Subsequent births tend to be a bit quicker, but by then the parents have some experience and are unlikely to leave things too late. Of course, rather than take such a chance not a few women turn up at the hospital or ring for the midwife when in false labour, but that is no great disgrace.

Most mothers feel thoroughly fed up, even irritated and indignant, if the baby seems to be *overdue*. The estimated date of delivery, calculated by adding 10 days to the date of the first day of the last monthly period, and then adding nine months to that, is accurate within a fortnight for four women out of five. So it is a useful estimate, but by no means a certain birthday. For women whose periods are not very regular, or whose memory for their periods is not very accurate, the E.D.D. can easily be a month out. If the dates conflict with the size of the womb as felt by the midwife or doctor, then the size is probably the better guide. A baby which is genuinely overdue, i.e. which has been in the womb for more than 42 weeks, is designated postmature. Postmaturity matters to the baby because the afterbirth may no longer meet its needs adequately, and it certainly causes the mother to fret and wonder how much longer the pregnancy can possibly last. The doctor is then very likely to say, 'Well, if you haven't gone into labour by next Friday we'll start it off for you', which is a great relief. Of course, the doctor will need to be pretty sure that the baby is overdue, for otherwise he might be inducing labour prematurely. Babies are ready to come into the world when they've been in the womb for about 40 weeks, and it is not to their advantage to make their entrance a month or so too soon.

The 'fed up' feeling at the end of pregnancy sometimes amounts to actual *depression*. High hormone levels may be one cause and there may be misgivings about the ordeal of labour and the extra responsibility when the baby is out of the womb. At a deeper psychological level, there may be a sense that something valuable is to be lost from the self, even though it will be discovered again in another, the infant. Sometimes this depression—often accompanied by an increase in anxiety—continues after the child's birth as puerperal or post-partum depression (see Chapter 11). Yet it has also been said that women who feel quite elated at the end of pregnancy are liable to depression after the birth, the suggestion being that their mood is *elevated* by the hormones secreted by the placenta or afterbirth, and then drops right down as the hormone levels drop sharply with the loss of the afterbirth in the third stage of labour.

In truth, despite these pointers it is very hard to predict from her state in pregnancy just how a woman will be after she's had her baby. Those who seem most troubled may do very well. Those whose pregnancies are trouble-free may be in grave difficulties with their baby, or may cope quite as well after the birth as before.

A useful application of elation at the end of pregnancy is energetic preparation for the baby's arrival, spring cleaning the house and collecting necessary supplies—a cot, bedding, nappies, tissues, towels, unisex clothes. This is sometimes referred to as the 'nesting instinct', and maybe it derives in part from the nesting drive of lower mammals. On the other hand, some mothers will not tempt providence by getting anything for the baby until it is born.

Now is as good a time as any to consider why, despite the high level of anxiety during pregnancy, the other disturbances of mood and the occasional quirks of behaviour, pregnant women are protected from admission to psychiatric wards.

One reason, I am sure, is the high level of tolerance for pregnant women. As a psychiatrist I am well aware of how angry and rejecting families can feel towards those members who are mentally ill. But allowances are made for the pregnant woman, firstly because any disorder she shows can easily be attributed to the pregnancy, secondly because the E.D.D. gives an indication that however awful she may be to live with now all should be well again by, say, next February, and thirdly because she is taken less for granted, and regarded somewhat differently—is valued, indeed, more highly—because of the exciting promise of the unknown little being she contains.

Another reason is the high level of interest, attention and support she receives through the pregnancy, not only from her family, but also from her general practitioner and the antenatal clinic. The importance of the other women as well as the staff at the clinic has already been described in the last chapter. It helps tremendously, if one is emotionally disturbed, to find that there are so many others in the same boat.

Though admissions to psychiatric wards are rare in pregnancy, admissions to maternity beds are not, and these are sometimes for predominantly emotional reasons. Some obstetricians seem more comfortable with the mechanics than the emotional overtones of childbearing (though the International Society for Psychosomatics in Obstetrics and Gynaecology, which is greatly concerned with the psychology of pregnancy, delivery and the period after, has obstetricians as well as psychiatrists in its huge membership) but nevertheless admit a woman during pregnancy for reasons which have more to do with the state of her mind than the physical complication which is the pretext for the admission. For example, tension may have to do with high blood pressure, extremely mixed feelings about pregnancy sometimes contribute to excessive vomiting, and the mother's depressed, demoralized state of mind or unsatisfactory social circumstances may well persuade the doctor to admit for a minor complication where otherwise he would not.

However, all those reasons do not account for the virtual absence of *serious* psychiatric disorder during pregnancy. This is a mystery as yet unexplained.

Finally, I would like to pass on some tips based upon some research by American workers (the Gordons) who found that certain changes in the behaviour of mothers-to-be were significantly associated with good social, psychological and marital adjustment after the baby's birth.

a) Make friends with couples with young children.
b) Make tidying the house less important.
c) Arrange some experienced help with the baby.
d) Get your husband to stay at home more.
e) Reduce social activities outside the home but don't cut them out.
f) Continue your outside interests but cut down on your responsibilities (this is not a good time to become secretary of the Mothers' Union, to start your own Women's Liberation Group, become a Samaritan or a

Marriage Guidance Counsellor, or play Lady Macbeth for your local drama group!).

g) Go to antenatal classes, and take your husband with you.
h) Try not to move house within six months before or after the birth—you need familiar surroundings and to know your local contacts.
i) Arrange baby sitters well ahead!

All this sounds like common sense and it is. The point is that the Gordons found that those who actually did those things fared rather better than those who did not.

7

Into Labour

Long before the start of labour, of course, a decision will have been reached about where to have the baby, *in hospital or at home*. This decision will be strongly influenced by people other than the parents, for example, there are circumstances under which doctors and midwives would be very reluctant to have anything to do with a home confinement.

The advantages of having a baby *at home* are obvious. The surroundings are totally familiar, and all the worries about when to go into hospital are relieved. There is no hanging about in the first stage of labour—the mother can keep herself usefully occupied right up till the last minute. Consequently the labour seems shorter than in hospital. If she already has children, she does not have to be parted from them, and even if they are taken off to Granny's for a few days this is less unsettling for them as they know their mother is at home. When a very young child loses his mother to a hospital for a week or more (which can seem like for ever to the child's mind) and then she returns with a baby, he has a lot with which to contend. There is no strange routine for the mother to cope with at home. The atmosphere can be delightfully free and easy, with friends and family drifting in and out and sharing very naturally in the birth. The husband's presence can be taken for granted and she will not be likely to find herself alone. Any favoured method of 'natural' childbirth can be used without inhibitions or restrictions. The mother will not be observed by strangers, and will not be disturbed by mini-dramas affecting other women; the privacy of the home is very precious. She can spend as much time as she likes with her baby, in any way she chooses, with no interference from anybody. Home is the ideal, but not the only, setting for 'childbirth with joy'.

To have her baby at home, a woman should be in her second or third pregnancy, with no present or past serious complications. She should not be younger than seventeen, older than thirty-five, or shorter than five feet. (Little women are more at risk of having difficult labours, even though the size of the baby is generally geared to the size of the womb in which it finds herself.) She must have a companion—husband, lover, mother, mother-in-law, sister, friend—to hand, she must have someone (such as a Home Help) to do the housework, and the services of a midwife and a doctor, backed up, if necessary, by a 'Flying Squad' from the local obstetric unit. She needs a spacious bedroom, separate from the rest of the household, a bed accessible from either side, adequate heating and hot running water.

The main snag of home confinements is that they are simply not as safe as deliveries in hospital. People snort at statistics, and quote their grandmother who had fourteen children at home, only lost one, and lived till she was 87. However, such anecdotes are statistically meaningless. They certainly go to show that home confinement is not desperately unsafe (though some might argue that the loss of one baby in fourteen is excessive) but they do not alter the fact that the risk of mother or baby's death is far less for hospital than for home confinements if like is compared with like. The reasons why maternal deaths are so creditably low in the Western world are not only a higher standard of living, but also the high quality of antenatal care and the excellent standard of hospital obstetrics. There is less justification for complacency in the perinatal mortality rate for the infant, but again, while the great majority of babies survive whether born at home or in hospital, their chances are significantly higher in hospital.

Home confinement is undoubtedly very attractive to many mothers, and they should certainly have the choice if they are having a second or third baby and are not disqualified for any of the reasons set out on page 62. But hospital is safer. Another disadvantage of home confinement is that the mother may be lured back to her domestic role before she has had time to get used to her new baby. In hospital she can, despite the distractions of communal living in an institution, focus on the baby who has been inside her for so long and has just come out, and know that for the time being she has no other responsibilities. At home, though, it is all too easy for her to say, 'Oh, I'll get it', 'Let me do it' and find herself an over-loaded willing horse, who soon feels somewhat less than willing, but lumbered. Obviously, a husband who has been able to take time off work, and who makes it his task to see that his wife is, at least for the first week, bothered with nothing but the baby (and who does his share of cuddling and nappy changing) will prevent such exploitation.

Incidentally, the conclusion I reached from one small piece of research is that not all women who seek to have their babies at home do so because they feel that home is the perfect place for so nice, natural and normal a happening. Some are simply scared stiff of hospital. The thought of being away from home in such a strange place puts them in a panic and, frightened as they are of the labour, hospital frightens them more.

Some women regard *hospital* as part of what has been called the 'medicalization of motherhood'. Stated baldly this view is that childbirth was an essentially natural, normal process until men got into the act and started to interfere, with their episiotomies (making a cut to let the baby's head out more easily) and forceps deliveries and anaesthesia and inductions, and their clever gadgets and gimmicks which turn a simple, emotionally satisfying process which has, after all, kept mankind going for millions of years, into a technological circus with the doctor as ringmaster. There is some truth in this. One looks in vain through the vast majority of textbooks by male obstetricians for more than a page or two about the mother's thoughts and feelings, though the accounts of the physiology, pathology and therapeutics of childbirth are generally excellent. On the other hand women writing about childbirth mainly from the viewpoint of users rather than providers of the service, have a striking tendency to put feelings first. Men, it might be argued, have brought safety to childbirth but little soul.

Such an argument would, I think, have held more water twenty years ago than now. Among today's foremost obstetricians are many (I will not embarrass them by naming names) outstandingly empathic, caring and humane men and (rightly) women. Safety is very important, to mothers as well as to doctors and midwives, and the huge change in the proportion of home to hospital confinements over the last 50 years (from 15 per cent in 1927 to about 90 per cent now) could hardly have taken place in the teeth of women's resolute opposition. My own birth as my parents' first child in a rented house in Wallington would be unthinkable now. Most women prefer to be delivered in hospital because they feel more secure there. If anything goes wrong, all necessary help is easily to hand. And over recent years hospital staff have recognized increasingly the emotional needs of the women in their charge. Antenatal classes have become more realistic, hospital routines a shade more relaxed, fathers are given a place they were previously denied, midwives seem less bossy and dogmatic and—dare I say it?—bitchy than they sometimes used to be, and doctors are just a little more likely to explain what they are doing. The mother is allowed freer access to her new baby, and the importance of 'bonding' is more often recognized. There is still much room for improvement especially, I think, in understanding women's negative or 'anti' attitudes and feelings rather than simply reacting unfavourably to them, but a little progress has been made towards bringing some of the best features of home confinement into hospital. Some of the misgivings mothers may have about hospitals I have mentioned already (p. 31–3, 46). To these I would add the widespread lack of privacy at what is a very private and intimate time in a woman's life, and the exposure to other women in labour which can be decidedly discouraging. (An acquaintance of mine went happily into hospital, was delighted to meet one of her old friends there, but felt decidedly queasy when the friend took one look at her and was promptly sick!).

Some suggest that the best compromise between the safety of hospital and the pleasures of a home confinement is the one- or two-day admission used by busy obstetric units rather than the more usual 7–10 days. However, though safety is thus ensured, I suspect that the other main advantage of a hospital delivery—the time to devote oneself more or less exclusively to the baby for a week or so—is lost, while the main snag of birth at home (apart from its being less safe)—that too much may be expected by one's family too soon—is not eliminated. In other words, in some respects the woman who comes into hospital for a very short time may have the worst of both worlds. However, there are all sorts and conditions of women, and some may be best suited by such an arrangement.

Labour is traditionally regarded as having *three stages.* The *first* is the gradual opening up of the cervix, or lower end of the womb, until it is wide enough to let the baby's head pass through. This dilation is achieved by the successive contractions of the womb, ever more frequent and longer. The *second* stage is that in which, by an irresistible impulse to bear down, the mother pushes her baby out through the lower end of the womb and the vagina into the breathing world. And the *third* stage is the delivery of the afterbirth.

Labour begins on average 40 weeks, or 280 days, from the beginning of the last monthly period. Actually, though, conception takes place at the time of ovulation which is about 14 days after the start of the period in a woman whose cycle runs 28 days. For most women with shorter or longer cycle, the E.D.D. may have to be put back, or forward, by a week. The E.D.D. is, in any case, so approximate that all that can be said with confidence is that 85 per cent of women have their babies within two weeks of that date. The actual time of onset of labour may be determined by a hormone secreted by the placenta or afterbirth.

Apart from the often overlooked 'show' and the occasional breaking of the waters, when the amniotic sac ruptures early rather than late, the chief and surest sign of the onset of labour is regular, sometimes painful, contractions of the womb. The effect of these is to pull up and dilate the cervix or canal at the lower end of the womb so that the baby's head can pass through. Progress in the first stage of labour is measured not only by the frequency and durations of contractions (which can be monitored very accurately with special apparatus in hospital), but also by the dilation of the cervix. This is gauged by a vaginal examination. At first the cervix will admit one finger, then two, then three. When it is half dilated it is felt as a rim round the baby's head. When it is fully dilated the rim has gone and only the head can be felt. The cervix must dilate to a diameter of just under 10 cm to let the head through.

The view of Dr Grantly Dick-Read, whose name is immortally associated with natural childbirth, was that fear causes tension in labour, tension pain, pain greater fear, and so by a vicious circle labour is rendered unnecessarily *prolonged* and painful. Instead of lying back and relaxing between contractions the tense woman remains on edge, shattered by the last pain and dreading the next. Her fears are largely determined by what she has heard of childbirth as an ordeal from other women. His admirable ideal was to take fear away and let nature take its course. You may be wondering, what is a prolonged labour? I was taught at Guy's Hospital that the sun should not set twice on a woman in labour, and although that seems a long time ago, and the wording may sound a little archaic, I believe that the sentiment still holds good.

There is good evidence to support Dr Dick-Read's contentions in respect of concealed anxiety. Research has shown that women free from anxiety, or women at least able to admit to it, are less likely to have a lengthy and difficult first stage of labour than 'stiff upper lip' women who feel anxious but acknowledge what they feel. This suggests that an important component of 'natural' childbirth may be the ability to be honest about one's feelings. 'Uptight' women (and how marvellously evocative that word is!) are likely to be 'uptight' in labour, and to have a hard time of it.

These days it is very easy to bring a woman's labour on at a more convenient time than 'nature' has determined. *Induction* is achieved by rupturing the membranes and releasing the amniotic fluid. A sharp object or a pair of forceps is pushed up through the cervix, and the membranes are (painlessly) torn. The loss of fluid (making 'the waters' break) alters the pressure within the womb, and consequently labour starts. Or a drug which stimulates the womb to contract may be used, e.g. syntocinin, which is usually given by a drip into one of the veins from a bottle of fluid in which it has been diluted, but can also be administered by mouth. Or labour may be induced by the use of hormones: the prostaglandins, which are used for late terminations of pregnancy can also be used to initiate labour, and are often given by mouth.

These methods have replaced the old fashioned (and

highly unreliable) techniques of castor oil purgation, a warm enema and a hot bath, all of which could well leave the mother-to-be exhausted and not necessarily in labour.

Why induce? There may be good medical reasons, such as toxaemia, when the blood supply to the baby from the afterbirth may not be sufficient, or Rhesus incompatibility when the level of the mother's antibodies to the baby's red blood cells may justify ending the pregnancy as soon as there is a reasonable chance that the baby will survive, rather than let it continue till it is likely to be jaundiced and anaemic at the time of birth. Postmaturity is another good medical reason for induction.

Far more controversy has been aroused by inductions simply for the convenience of mother, midwife or obstetrician. Obviously it is nice to have the baby at a time which suits one, provided that no extra danger ensues. It may be nice, too, and reassuring, to have one's obstetrician in attendance, eager and on the ball during the daytime rather than bleary eyed at night. (There is no night shift for doctors: if they are 'on call' then they can be called out at night after a day's work, and have to work through the next day too.) Provided the pregnancy is very near to term such a procedure is remarkably safe, and there is little evidence that such 'flying in the face of nature' is punished by more difficult or painful labour or less healthy babies than labours which are not induced. This is very much a matter for personal choice—the choice, unless there are strong medical indications, being that of the mother. Induction should never be carried out simply for the convenience of staff, but where the mother wants it, it can be a great boon.

The woman who is going into hospital (and that is bound to be the majority of my readership) had better be prepared as her hour draws nigh. She will need to have packed, or ready to hand, up to three nightdresses, a dressing gown and slippers, a plentiful supply of pants, and a pair of nursing brassieres (allowing access to the nipples). Although the hospital provides sanitary towels, it is no bad idea to have a personal store of a dozen. Of course, all these are in addition to the usual toilet requisites. As time may hang heavy on the hands, something to read and writing materials are likely to be welcomed. One or two small personal belongings may help to make a tiny corner of hospital a little like home. Old teddies are precious to some. Others will not be parted from their mascots, especially at so fraught a time. (To my mind, though, the trouble with mascots is that they may get lost, and then all the superstitious fears they ward off erupt!)

The time to go into hospital is when the womb is contracting regularly, if the waters have broken or if there has been a show. Any doubt about what to do can readily be discussed with the sister or nurse in charge of the maternity ward, over the telephone. She is very experienced in assessing such situations, and is available throughout the twenty-four hours.

Transport to the hospital must be arranged unless it is just round the corner. This either means sending for an ambulance or driving a private car. Those who have a car available to them may well wish to use it rather than wait for the ambulance, but had better make sure it is roadworthy, reliable, and contains enough petrol. On the whole women in labour are well advised not to drive themselves into hospital!

Arrangements will have to be made to keep things going at home while the mother is in hospital. If she is not sure that these are satisfactory, she will fret while she is away. This is a situation where grandparents can come splendidly into their own, if willing and readily available, particularly in looking after any young children already in the family. If there are no children the husband should be able to take care of himself, but a grandmother, sister,

sister-in-law, friend or neighbour is invaluable if able to see to the house and do a little cleaning, cooking and shopping, while he is still at work. If he is going to take some time off the best time may be when his wife first comes home with the baby.

8

Delivery

Once the first stage of labour is over the baby's head can pass into the upper part of the vagina. As it does so the mother experiences an irresistible impulse to 'bear down' and push with all her might to expel her baby through the length of the vagina and out, by way of the vulva, into the outside world. Very often the onset of the second stage is marked by the desire to vomit as well as the 'bearing down' feeling. During the first stage of labour little or no absorption takes place from the stomach, so it is not a good idea to prepare for labour with a hearty meal. Should an anaesthetic be needed, there is always a risk that stomach contents could flood the lungs, causing a very dangerous inhalation pneumonia.

The *second stage* lasts up to an hour in women going into labour for the first time, and for much less than that in those who have had a baby before. Contractions of the upper part of the womb continue, at a rate of about one every two minutes, lasting for about a minute. These involuntary efforts to push the baby out are considerably assisted by voluntary action, holding the breath and straining massively as if to open the bowels. Panting between pushes allows a brief rest. Because the bowels may indeed be opened at the time under this gigantic effort, an enema may be given early in labour to clear them before the second stage. As the baby's head approaches the perineum, or tissue between the legs, it sometimes seems to the woman in labour that her previous fantasy of being split in two is indeed being realized. While this cannot, of course, happen, the trick of getting the baby's head through the slit of the vulva is not always pulled off, and the skin of the perineum may indeed be split, and require stitching after labour is over. To forestall this, to facilitate delivery and to ensure that the split occurs in a place which is convenient and easy to suture a cut (or episiotomy) is often made when the perineum is tightly stretched by the baby's head. When so tightly stretched the skin of the perineum is partly anaesthetized, but a local anaesthetic is always injected before the cut is made.

The baby's head usually presents crown first, and by the time the vulva is distended to 3 or 4 cm the back of the neck is level with and just behind the front of the mother's pelvis, while the face is towards the mother's bottom. The head is then delivered by extension of the baby's head, which the midwife assists while the mother is discouraged from bearing down. The midwife to some extent holds the head back, so as to ease the baby's passage into the world and prevent it from being too quick. As the head extends the face looks out, and there is the opportunity to wipe it and suck out fluid from the nose, mouth and throat, for breathing is about to begin.

After the delivery of the head, the biggest and widest part of a newborn baby, all should be plain sailing. The baby's shoulders now turn in the mother's pelvis, so that the baby now looks to right or left rather than downwards (if the mother is presumed to be on her back during this stage of labour), and after a short pause the womb's contractions resume. With further bearing down first one shoulder appears, then the other, and the rest of the baby is delivered by lifting him upwards so that at last he can be seen by the mother.

Babies are no longer spanked into breathing, but they are held upside down (a position to which they are well used) or lain down and any fluid is again sucked out of the nose, mouth and throat, so that there is no obstacle to breathing, and when breathing starts there is little risk that fluid will be inhaled into the baby's lungs. He may well start breathing with a cry, which might sound sad, but is encouraging to one and all that he is well and truly alive, and making his presence felt. In fact crying is a very healthy use of the lungs, and expands them to the full. As he sucks in air his colour changes from a slightly disconcerting blue to an agreeable pink, or an uncompromising red. (No research has been carried out on whether a predominance of any of these colours is related to future political leanings!)

The umbilical cord which joins the baby to the afterbirth and through which till now he has received his oxygen and nourishment and passed out his waste products is now clamped, severed and tied. That phase of existence is over, and soon we only have an umbilicus, navel or 'belly button' to remind us that it ever happened. The cord is cut after the last pulsation of blood from the afterbirth is felt to reach the baby. It is cut and tied partly to prevent the baby losing blood from leakage back, and partly to stop the mother losing blood via the afterbirth.

The second stage of labour is now over, and the *third* is about to begin—the delivery of the afterbirth. If nature is allowed to take its course, the womb rests for quarter of an hour, then starts contracting again and pushes the afterbirth out by the end of another quarter of an hour, usually without great effort compared with the exertion of the second stage.

Usually these days, however, the third stage is hurried on by giving the mother an injection at the time that the baby's shoulder appears, to cause contraction of the womb straight after the baby has been born. By pulling on the umbilical cord the midwife or doctor can then withdraw the placenta and complete the third stage in about five minutes. This procedure is not to get labour over and done with as soon as possible but to forestall bleeding from the womb, which can be a troublesome complication of the third stage. The afterbirth is carefully examined, mainly to ensure that no bits have been left behind, which could cause bleeding or infection later, and the birth is completed. Occasionally babies are born in a 'caul': the waters not having broken, the bag of amniotic fluid is intact. Legend has it that such babies will never die of drowning (though if they were not at once released from the bag they would, there and then!).

When Sir James Simpson introduced *anaesthesia to obstetrics* in 1847 he was not universally regarded as a benefactor of womankind. Many pointed out (chiefly, I believe, men, and women past childbearing age) that it is stated in Genesis: 'In sorrow shalt thou bring forth children'. Consequently to relieve the pain was to contravene the will of the (Old Testament) God. However when Queen Victoria in 1853 consented to be administered chloroform for the birth of Prince Leopold, and expressed herself well satisfied with its effects, 'chloroform à la reine' had the seal of royal approval and became more generally acceptable. Even so, the *relief of pain* during childbirth is still a matter of controversy, and rightly so, for the issues are not clear-cut, nor are all women in labour alike.

I don't think anyone would dispute that anaesthesia and analgesia have a very important place in obstetrics. (Analgesia, by the way, means the relief of pain, anaesthesia the abolition of sensation. Aspirin is an analgesic, ether an anaesthetic. All anaesthetics abolish pain along with other sensation. A general anaesthetic causes unconsciousness, while a local anaesthetic, given by injection or a spray, deadens all sensation in a particular area.) There are arguments, however, about how frequently drugs and anaesthetics should be used, which ones, at whose bidding (the mother's or the midwife's), about any risks to the mother or her baby, and whether the experience of childbirth is improved or spoilt by their use. There is no simple answer to any of these questions.

Tranquillizers may be used early in the first stage of labour if the mother is especially anxious. This is neither analgesia nor anaesthesia but if fear and tension are allayed so, to some extent, will be pain. Tranquillizers do not impair consciousness, and though unlikely to be accepted by women trained in natural childbirth, are unlikely to do harm, and may well be beneficial to those who are beginning to regard the labour as an ordeal. Valium is now the tranquillizer in most common use.

Sedatives have an action intermediate between tranquillizers and hypnotics (or sleeping tablets). They calm, but at the cost of causing some drowsiness. They can help an anxious woman to drowse through the early contractions of the first stage, but will upset the rhythm of the mother who wants to be in harmony with labour and to use her consciousness for active relaxation and controlled breathing.

Labour can often last all through the night, and there is no reason why a woman should not sleep for some of this time. Indeed, it will help considerably for her to be well rested for the rigours of the second stage. A *hypnotic* (or sleeping tablet), often the same drug as a sedative but in higher dosage, may ensure sleep where otherwise there would be a tense and frightened wakefulness throughout a long night. On the other hand, a sleeping tablet does not remove pain, and some women who were prepared for natural childbirth find themselves at a loss in coping with contractions if they are woken by pain but still half doped.

In practice, sedatives have been virtually replaced by tranquillizers, but hypnotics are still widely used. The most popular is nitrazepam which is very similar to the tranquillizer Valium, and is less likely than most other sleeping tablets to cause undue drowsiness on waking. Unless labour is prolonged all such drugs are best given earlier rather than later in the first stage, so that the mother is awake, refreshed, when the greatest demands are to be made on her.

Pethedine, a true *analgesic*, is a very popular drug in the first stage of labour. Given by injection it acts within quarter of an hour for up to four hours. If given too early it may slow labour up, but when contractions are well established it makes them much less painful. It can also produce a happy, relaxed 'top of the world' feeling which is all to the good. It is particularly useful for women having their first babies. Some, however, find that it makes them unpleasantly drowsy, and less in control of themselves than they want to be.

An important point which must be made is that all the drugs so far mentioned, and all general anaesthetics, enter the mother's blood stream and thus the baby's. There is therefore the risk that the baby will be somewhat drugged at birth, which is obviously undesirable. The ideal pain reliever is wholly effective, lasts as long as but no longer than is wanted for its particular purpose, has no side-effects (in particular no drowsiness) and leaves the baby quite unaffected. Such a perfect preparation has yet to be discovered.

Can pain be relieved *without the use of drugs*? Well, the techniques of *'natural' childbirth* and *psychoprophylaxis* enable the mother to relax and control her breathing, sometimes taking very deep breaths, at others frequent, shallow, gasping ones, in such a way that she can, as it were, float with the tide of her womb's contractions, rather than defy them like Queen Canute, or be submerged. Her spouse can be taught to rub her back and thighs (where the pain of the contractions is often felt) so as to rub them away, which is rewarding for him and very nice for his wife. Sheila Kitzinger describes how an awed surrender to the power of the womb's contractions can give a sensual pleasure akin to that of making love.

Hypnotism is an excellent method of freeing a woman from awareness of any pain while keeping her wholly conscious, and of course, it does not in the least affect the baby. Its use is limited more by the lack of doctors and midwives trained and confident in hypnosis than any shortage of suitable subjects. A certain amount of auto-suggestion or self hypnosis is, I think, an essential part of 'natural' childbirth.

Turning to more traditional methods, I must welcome the tried and trusted *gas and oxygen* machine, a staunch friend for many years to women in labour. The gas is nitrous oxide or laughing gas, mixed half and half with oxygen, and administered by the woman herself, holding the mask to her face and breathing deeply. In the first stage of labour she takes deep breaths of the mixture as soon as the womb starts to contract (her husband can feel this with his hand before she is aware of it) thus fore-stalling the painful climax. There is no need to inhale the mixture between contractions. In the second stage, when it is necessary to bear down when the womb contracts, the technique is to take several deep breaths just before the next contraction is expected.

Although gas is a general anaesthetic when administered this way it is most unlikely to cause unconsciousness. It is very safe to mother and baby, and quite pleasant and effective. Alternative methods of inhalation anaesthesia are *Trilene* or *Penthrane*, which are both mixed with air rather than oxygen.

Regional, or *local* anaesthesia abolishes pain and all other sensation from the womb, vagina and perineum, enabling the woman to remain alert and interested, able to breathe and bear down in accordance with the phase of her labour, but in some ways more of an onlooker than an active participant in the birth. Local anaesthesia does not affect the baby. The best known and most fashionable these days is *epidural* anaesthesia, in which an injection given into the base or tip of the spine deadens the nerves carrying sensation from the area into the spinal cord. The technique is a skilled one, but safe and effective. However, it often inhibits 'bearing down', and a forceps delivery is commonly required. An interesting objection to analgesia, raised by the psychoanalyst Helen Deutsch, is surprisingly consistent with the Old Testament dictum: 'In sorrow shalt thou bring forth children'. This is that women have a *psychological need to suffer*, and that without suffering they may feel uneasy and dissatisfied with the experience of childbirth. Indeed, if they haven't suffered by the time the baby is born, they may well suffer afterwards from nagging fears that the baby will not develop properly or even survive, or they may become depressed.

However, I have not come across any evidence that those who do suffer so are less likely to have misgivings about their baby or be depressed in the post-partum period than those who do not. Female masochism is to my mind largely a myth, and no justification at all for denying any woman the relief of her pain in childbirth.

Ms. Deutsch's other objections are more valid, and have been voiced by many others. These are that anaesthesia reduces a woman's pride in her achievement, her satisfaction in the active participation in the spontaneous labour, and her ecstatic rediscovery of the baby within her as it emerges into the outside world. Women who particularly fear losing control or dying in labour may well be more frightened still by the impairment of consciousness which often accompanies the relief of pain.

I can certainly add, from my own practice, that some women who experience childbirth without any pain at all, because of epidural analgesia, or who through Caesarian section are denied the experience of childbirth altogether, feel that they have 'cheated', or are not proper women. There is misgiving about having got off too lightly (which *is* somewhat masochistic) a sense of having missed a great experience, or by-passed an initiation rite which would allow them to feel at one with the body of mature, mothering women. Other mothers, I'm afraid, are all too likely to reinforce these feelings by snooty or catty ploys in 'one-upmanship'.

Towards the end of the twentieth century there can hardly be any doubt that when Sir James Simpson introduced anaesthesia for childbirth he did women the greatest possible service, and that the developments and refinements of the past 130 years have not only meant that all sorts of complications can be dealt with in complete safety, but that no woman need now suffer unduly in her labour. At the same time women in labour differ one from another as much as people do at other times, and what suits one very well may not be what another wants at all. Those who have never experienced labour need guidance as to what they may expect, and what the various drugs, analgesics and anaesthetics may do for them. Those who have had a baby or two may still not know everything, or may not recall their previous labours very clearly or accurately, so they too need guidance. However, when she knows the score it is a woman's right to decide if she wants to do with or without analgesia, or to leave the management of her labour to the midwives and doctors. Labour is a very individual experience, and although the professionals and experts generally know best, and are far more often right than the amateurs, even they cannot know just how it will feel to a particular woman. So the choice should be hers, with every right to change her mind if she regrets what she has chosen; happily modern obstetric analgesia is generally sufficiently flexible to allow that.

The *mother's love* for her baby is, as I have said already, an enormous help in the early days, weeks, months, even years of the child's life, turning what is otherwise a heavy and demanding duty into a continual source of pleasure and delight. I have mentioned that the mother's self-esteem in pregnancy, her justifiable love for herself and the baby inside her, may be an important component of mother-love. I shall have more to say about the mother child relationship later (Chapters 10–13) but must now discuss the impact that the first sight of her baby has on the mother, and the effect this is likely to have on the love the mother feels. The phenomenon of *imprinting* is familiar to many from Konrad Lorenz's book about grey-lag geese, *King Solomon's Ring*, and to still more from a delightful Tom and Jerry cartoon, in which the first person a chick sees on breaking out of its shell is Tom the cat, whom it instantly greets with the cry, 'That's my mummy.' Tom is quite prepared to exploit the situation, as he fancies a tasty chicken dinner, but despite the repeated warnings of Jerry the mouse, the chick remains steadfastly loyal. In the end, you'll be glad to be reminded, even Tom's crafty feline heart is melted. Lorenz describes how geese who first saw him, rather than their actual mothers, similarly seemed to accept and respond to him as if he were the mother.

It is doubtful that anything very similar happens to human babies, which are relatively much less developed and consequently less able to register and subsequently recognize another being, but nevertheless the feeling has got about that the moment of birth is a highly significant instinctual as well as psychological and biological event. However, as the baby is so underdeveloped and immature, the greater importance is attributed to the mother's rather than her infant's experience of the critical moment.

The suggestion is, then, that the more alert a mother is at the time she gives birth, the sooner she sees her baby and the more she has to do with him then, the stronger will be her bond of mother-love. Consequently mothers who are anaesthetized for a forceps delivery or a Caesarian section, who are too drowsy to be properly aware of the birth or who have puny babies who need to go straight into special care, are said to have more difficulty in feeling that their babies are really theirs, and in loving them.

Dr Marshall Klaus of the Case Western Reserve University, Cleveland, Ohio, has shown that babies cuddled by their mothers in the first minutes of life will be healthier in some ways, kissed more and scolded less in later life than those who are not.

There is a growing recognition that the emotional needs of the mother in respect of her new baby may require special consideration at the time of delivery. The fashionable views of the French obstetrician, Frederick Leboyer, are worth mentioning here, for though fashions come and go (and come back again) at a great speed in midwifery, and though some of what he believes seems pretty far-fetched, yet he is having an influence on labour room procedure which many women welcome.

The Leboyer approach, based upon recollections, through psychoanalysis, of the trauma of his own birth might be caricatured: 'Be Nice to the Newborn', or 'Babies have Feelings Too'. There can be little doubt that birth is a huge stress for the baby. There it is, warm, wet and cosy in the quiet dark, all its needs met by the blood supply through the umbilical cord. Then, after hours under the most extreme pressure, it is squeezed through the vagina and thrust spluttering, without bearings, and relatively alone into a cold, bright, noisy world where it is surrounded by air rather than fluid. Small wonder that the baby so often greets this world with an angry cry!

Leboyer's technique involves delivering the baby into a hushed and darkened room, not immediately cutting the umbilical cord (which he regards as an extra source of oxygen for a few minutes after the birth) then placing the infant on the mother's abdomen, as close as possible to where it has been lying inside, and stroking it, slowly, gently and with love. The bustle and boisterousness of the usual birth is transformed into a quiet, leisurely, relaxed, twilit occasion which lessens the shock of the baby's arrival. Until the moment of birth all noise has been muffled by the fluid in which the baby lies, so voices should be low. His skin is unused to any rough material but the skin of his mother's abdomen is unlikely to chafe, and when he has been removed from there he is given a warm bath, to imitate somewhat the conditions of the womb and wean him rather than thrust him into the world. The stroking movements when he lies on his mother are designed to imitate the subtle contractions of the womb before birth, and help him to feel more at home.

Objections to Leboyer are firstly that his recollections of his own birth are likely to be fantasy, as it is highly improbable that, at birth, the nervous system and the capacity to be aware of the self are sufficiently developed to make much sense of the experience, pleasant or otherwise. However, this resembles a 'the hook doesn't really hurt the fish' argument and is not a very strong reason for not trying to be humane to the newborn. It may more reasonably be argued that delay in cutting the umbilical cord, far from improving the supply of oxygen, may actually cause the baby to lose some blood back into the detaching, and no longer nourishing, afterbirth. The risks of chilling while lying on the mother's abdomen, and of losing the useful vermix or insulating covering of grease through bathing have also been mentioned. There are those (with whom I agree) who suggest that a more natural contact between mother and child at this time is for her to cuddle him to her breast, and others who feel that the mere six minutes' contact advocated by Leboyer are too meagre, and that up to an hour is more rewarding to mother and child. However, not a few mothers feel much too tired to hold their baby so soon after giving birth.

Some of us find the Leboyer mystique over-solemn, are disconcerted by his lack of scientific method, and see no reason why all that he preaches should be regarded as Holy Writ. At the same time, it is refreshing that an obstetrician should have reminded his colleagues that birth is a very important event for the baby, and that time should be set aside for mother and baby to meet.

To conclude this chapter, I shall mention the roles of the midwife and the husband at the time of delivery.

The *midwife* is a professional, specialist nurse who has taken the place of the woman who attends the mother in labour, in societies less advanced than our own, because she has had children herself.

She looms large in the life of the woman who is advanced in pregnancy, in labour, or newly delivered. The relationship is relatively short but intense. The midwife sees her client well and truly with her pants down. Finesse and social conventions are soon brushed aside in labour; at no other time are appearances less likely to be maintained. But while the mother is so exposed, physically and emotionally, the midwife, safe in her professional role, is controlled, calm, detached and knowledgeable. Consequently, despite the brevity of the involvement the woman in labour may in some ways see and react to the midwife as her mother. An awareness of the strength of the feelings projected on to her will enable the midwife to understand why she is regarded with such devotion or (occasionally) loathing without taking the feelings personally, to keep her head, and to remember that any careless, inconsiderate or thoughtless word or deed on her part can be far more hurtful than at a less critical time. Of course, not every woman regards the midwife as a mother-substitute, and many see her, rightly, as a professional who has a service to offer, of which they wish to make use, and nothing more. But the midwife unprepared for the odd outburst from her charge may react in a dismayed, affronted, rejecting or scornful way which will help neither of them.

The ability, without being sloppy, sentimental or insincere, to make that mother feel special, to make her welcome, and to regard her baby as an exciting and valuable new member of the human race, is precious. If she can feel that her labour has been worth while rather than that the baby was dragged out somehow despite her lack of co-operation, then the job has been well done. The good midwife gets the best from the mother she is helping, and makes her aware of it. She does not blame her for her faults, but reinforces her abilities. The good midwife is, in fact, a paragon, and happily there seem to be a lot of them around.

The *father* has graduated from the role of clown, buffoon or fall guy, his innocent, inept eagerness, as it were, in counterpoint to his wife's serenity and suffering, to a principal in the drama of delivery, rivalling the obstetrician for the position of male lead. In this country this change in attitude has taken place only in the last fifteen years or so, as part of the general transformation of social and sexual roles and behaviour. It now seems so natural and proper that the man should be involved in his woman's childbearing that his exclusion for so long seems bizarre.

Today's husband can be a great source of strength, comfort and encouragement. He can share the anxieties and anticipation of pregnancy with a view to taking an active part in the delivery as well as becoming a father. He can give moral support at the antenatal clinic and classes, can learn with his wife about the physiology and psychology of pregnancy and childbearing, and help her with breathing and relaxing exercises. Recognizing that she may need to take more from him emotionally during pregnancy, and give less, he can try to be loving and giving and derive satisfaction from managing to be tolerant and understanding. It will help both the couple if he can gain some insight into his misgivings about how the baby may affect his relationship with his wife, his twinges of jealousy, his resentment of her self absorption and any flagging in her sexual desire. He can't be compelled to be a saint, but a little saintliness goes a long way, and how good it makes him feel!

At the time of delivery his confirmation that labour appears to have started and his assistance in calling the hospital or midwife are invaluable. In hospital the presence of her husband means that no woman need ever fear being on her own. He is there with her to help her speak up for herself, or to do so for her provided he does not impose his own view on hers. She feels she has an ally and, if he does not see himself as a watchdog rather than an intermediary, he can be a staunch support without being at odds with the staff.

Remembering the exercises they have practised together he can help his wife to breathe slowly and deeply, or quickly and shallowly, and to relax. By rubbing the small of her back or her thighs he can ease her pains. By putting up with her tetchiness he can ease a potentially fraught situation and sustain her image of herself as doing a good job. And by encouraging her to bear down when the time comes, and to hold off when the head is about to be delivered even though her every instinct is to push as hard as she can, he can ease his child's passage into the world.

Not all husbands, of course, are up to all this and they needn't feel ashamed. Some are too nervous, uneasy, squeamish or queasy to cope with labour, and some wives would rather not have them present at a time when they are so utterly exposed, and their reservations should be respected. Some men are too touchy, defensive or belligerent to be at all comfortable in the hospital setting, and their wives, embarrassed by their attitude, may be more relaxed if they are out of the way! But for those who are able to witness their baby's birth there is a special reward, a sense of pride and wonder and tenderness and delight, which brings man and wife especially close, and gets the new phase of their relationship, parenthood, off to a flying start.

As a footnote, I will mention that of a group of 200 women I spoke to a few weeks after they had had their babies at The London Hospital, a quarter found the experience of delivery worse than they had expected, three-eighths found it better, a quarter felt that it was pretty much what they had expected, and the remaining eighth had either had Caesarian sections or could not remember how they had felt.

9

Complications

The complications of labour, though naturally feared by most women, are remarkably manageable in modern obstetric practice.

Sometimes the afterbirth is situated at the lower segment of the womb. There it prevents the baby's head from engaging in the pelvis, while the stretching of the lower part of the womb by the contractions before delivery causes partial detachment of the afterbirth from the wall and bleeding. Bleeding from the vagina in the later months of pregnancy is a warning of this condition called *placenta praevia*, which always necessitates admission to hospital until the baby is safely delivered, as there is bound to be further bleeding, especially at the onset of labour. Placenta praevia is one of the indications for a Caesarian section, but this is not always necessary. The time the mother spends waiting in hospital is bound to cause her apprehension, though the outcome is very likely to be happy.

Delay in labour is due to insufficient contraction of the womb, to the baby's being in an awkward position, or to narrowing or restriction of the passage through which the baby must pass (pelvis, vagina, perineum).

In the *first stage of labour* delay is usually due to insufficiency of the womb's contractions (see pp. 66–7). *Uterine inertia* may be due to under- or overactivity of the womb. *Underactivity* is shown by infrequent, irregular contractions which dilate the cervix or neck of the womb very slowly and uncertainly. The same measures as are used to induce labour, rupturing the membranes and giving a drug to stimulate the womb into regular contractions in a drip into a vein usually overcome the inertia and establish normal labour.

Overactivity (Hypertonic inertia) is more evidently related,' sometimes, to a psychological factor, namely anxiety, but may also be associated with the baby's lying at the back rather than the front of the womb. The contractions are short and sharp but inefficient. Sedation, or the relief of pain with pethedine or local analgesia are helpful, and syntocinin in a drip may be given too. All measures which allay anxiety such as knowledge of what is happening in labour, confidence in the staff team and the presence of the husband tend to reduce or eliminate the occurrence of this kind of inertia.

Disproportion between the width of the baby's head and the width of the pelvis causes delay. If the baby is very big (as it may be if for example the mother is diabetic) then it may be simply too big to go through the pelvis. On the other hand, if the pelvis is very small or deformed (as used to be a consequence of rickets) the baby cannot be born normally, and a Caesarian section will be needed. In either of these rare cases, the condition will have been detected at the antenatal clinic by the failure of the baby's head to engage in the pelvis, examination of the pelvis by vaginal examination and X-ray. Far more often disproportion is due to the baby's head being in an awkward position. To present the narrowest possible width to go through the pelvis, the back of the baby's head needs to be at the front, and the neck needs to be well bent so that the chin rests on the baby's chest. Even so there is a certain amount of moulding or overlap of the bones of the baby's skull (which are not fused together like those of the adult) to squeeze the head through. If the baby's head is not bent well forward, and if the back of the head is towards the back of the mother, there will be delay in the first stage, though the likelihood is that eventually the head will rotate so that the back is forwards, will then bend properly and normal delivery will take place.

The idea of disproportion must seem alarming to many mothers, conjuring up visions of being stuck in labour for days, getting weaker all the time, being seriously damaged, and, after all, losing the baby. But the natural course of labour, assisted by some gentle manipulation by the obstetrician overcomes most problems, and Caesarian section easily takes care of the rest.

Delay in the second stage of labour is recognized when, although the cervix is fully dilated, the head no longer descends. A second stage of more than an hour for a first baby, and more than half an hour for subsequent ones, is delayed.

The cause may be a weakly contracting womb after a long and tiring first stage or if the mother is over-sedated, in which case a forceps delivery is required.

There is rarely disproportion in the second stage of labour, when the baby's head is engaged in the pelvis, but the head may be temporarily stuck in an unsatisfactory position—the back of the head remaining at the back of the pelvis, or rotated halfway to the front and then stuck, or the head halfway extended so that the brow is the part coming out first, or wholly extended so that the face presents first. These problems are dealt with by the obstetrician's moving the head manually into a more satisfactory position, if necessary, and then completing the delivery with the aid of forceps. This is a simple enough matter, provided the obstetrician is readily available; this is one of the situations where it is a distinct advantage to be having the baby in hospital.

In older women having their first baby the floor of the pelvis or perineum—the tissues round the vulva or opening to the vagina—may not have much give, and may be an obstacle to the final delivery of the head. The answer to this is an episiotomy, or neat cut with scissors under local anaesthesia. Some obstetricians advocate a routine episiotomy, arguing that it avoids excessive stretching of the muscles of the pelvic floor and consequently hastens the return to a satisfactory sex life. This may not be a thought uppermost in the mind of the woman emerging from the second stage of labour (though for those happy few who find the experience a nigh orgasmic one it may!) but they may be very grateful for such consideration a few weeks later.

Distress of the baby or the mother during labour are indications for action. *Foetal* distress means that the baby is short of oxygen. This may be because the umbilical cord has become knotted, looped round the baby's neck or compressed between the baby's skull and the mother's pelvis, cutting off the blood supply. Or there may be trouble with the afterbirth, aggravated during labour by the contractions of the womb. During these the afterbirth is unable to deliver any blood, so the supply has to be made up between whiles, and if it is not working efficiently the oxygen then delivered to the baby may not be enough. Signs of foetal distress are irregularity or change in rate of the heart beat, detected by listening with a foetal stethoscope, or more obviously by a monitor; a green discharge from the mother's vagina, indicating that the baby has evacuated the thick green *meconium* in its rectum; or frantic movements, as though the baby were being asphyxiated, which indeed it is. All these indicate that if the baby is to be born alive and normal the birth must be speeded up. In the first stage of labour this is by Caesarian section, in the second by a forceps delivery.

The mother's distress may be physical or mental. *Physical distress*, comprising extreme shortness of breath and exhaustion, is likely to occur in those who are disabled by heart, lung, or kidney disease, for example, or diabetes. *Mental distress*—acute anxiety, depression and low morale—hardly needs explanation. A few unhappy, bewildered, mistrustful, weary and pain-racked women, often quite unprepared for the labour they have experienced, reach the second stage in such a state. The usual means of relieving such distress, be it physical or mental, is a forceps delivery.

What is a *forceps delivery*? It sounds rather grim, but is none the less a great boon to the mother, or baby, in difficulties in the second stage of labour. The instrument is in two parts, each of which is slid gently between the baby's head and the mother's pelvis before they are locked together in such a way that, stably and firmly, in a series of pulls, the baby's head is drawn out of the pelvis. The process takes place under anaesthesia, usually local. In the hands of an experienced obstetrician, a forceps delivery is swift and safe and, under local anaesthesia, can be as emotionally satisfying to the mother as a normal delivery. An alternative to forceps delivery is the vacuum extractor. By its means a vacuum is created in a metal cap applied to the crown of the baby's head. Traction, or pulling, is similar to that for a forceps delivery. The baby is left with a swelling at the site of the head which disappears within a few hours.

A *Caesarian* section used to be a desperate venture, cutting open the womb of a nigh dead mother to give her baby a chance of life. Julius Caesar was born this way, and hence the name. Now it is a very acceptable alternative to what might otherwise be a long, difficult, or even impossible labour, or where there is risk to the life of the baby or mother. In this country 6 per cent of babies are born this way. Under a general anaesthetic (given without the usual sedation beforehand, so that the baby will not be affected) an incision is made in the wall of the abdomen (often transversely and below the line of the pubic hair, so that when the hair grows again no scar is visible) and access to the womb is thus obtained. Another transverse incision is then made through the wall of the lower segment of the womb and through this the baby's head is delivered (after the bag of amniotic fluid in which it floats has been opened). The baby's eyes, nose and mouth are at once wiped and sucked clear of any mucus or fluid, and then the rest of the baby is delivered. Held upside down while the mouth and throat are again sucked clear, he or she should soon cry. The umbilical cord is tied and cut, the mother is given an injection of syntometrine which makes the womb contract strongly, and the afterbirth is then delivered through the same incision in the womb. When the womb is empty, the incision is carefully stitched up, as is the incision through the wall of the abdomen, and the operation is over, having taken three quarters of an hour or so.

The operation is so safe now because of the huge advances in surgical technique through this century, the comparable development and refinement of anaesthesia, the availability of blood for transfusion if necessary and the use of antibiotics to combat any infection. Also the baby stands a much better chance of survival, even if it has to be delivered prematurely (for example if a placenta praevia starts to bleed profusely) because of the high quality of care which can be given to tiny and puny babies.

Some women are rather happy to be spared the pain of labour, especially if they know beforehand that for good reasons a Caesarian section is to be performed. It is rather nice to be put to sleep and wake up and find your baby almost magically beside you. Others feel disappointed, cheated, not proper women, worried about having been cut open, about the scar and the possibility of a weakness in the womb, and particularly miss the thrill of having pushed their own baby out into the world, and met him at the moment of his birth. Also they don't like the discomfort of the wound and stitches in the early days after the operation. However (except perhaps in the more questionable private practices) Caesarian sections are never performed except for very good obstetric reasons—placenta praevia, disproportion, toxaemia, a previous history of Caesarian section, or of a very difficult labour, foetal distress in the first stage of labour—and so whatever the mother's emotional attitude or reaction, she is confronted with a real necessity, not a mere whim or fashion or self-indulgence. Recovery from the operation is very quick, and the woman who has had a 'Caesar' can be home as soon as the woman who has had a normal delivery. The risk that the scar in the womb will give way in a subsequent labour is remarkably low, so it is quite possible for a woman who has once had a Caesarian section to give birth normally later.

A dreaded complication of the third stage of labour used to be *post partum haemorrhage*. This resulted from insufficient contraction of the newly delivered womb, or from retention of part of the afterbirth, and was sometimes so swift and severe as to cause extreme shock, sometimes fatal, sometimes resulting in permanent damage to the pituitary gland at the base of the brain, (which controls all the other endocrine or hormone producing glands), and a condition known as Sheehan's syndrome. Nowadays if the womb is not contracted enough an extra injection of syntometrine is given, while if a piece of afterbirth has been retained it can easily be removed under general anaesthesia, and if blood loss has been excessive, it can always be replaced by transfusion.

Two particular kinds of problem delivery are breech and twins.

Breech delivery means that the baby presents bottom rather than head first. This is normal for the seventh or eighth months of pregnancy, but in the ninth the head should present and become engaged, so that the baby is born head first. Babies born prematurely may be breech deliveries, as may the second of twins. Any obstacle to the head's entering the pelvis may also result in a breech presentation. As it is generally easier and safer to deliver the baby head first, efforts are occasionally made to turn the baby in the last two months of pregnancy if the breech is found to be presenting. This can be due without anaesthesia in the antenatal clinic provided the mother is sufficiently relaxed. The doctor or midwife pushes the baby's body up one side of the abdomen and the head down the other, and usually the baby turns quite easily. If the head can then be made to engage, the baby will stay in the normal upside-down position. Otherwise the procedure may have to be repeated at a subsequent visit. Very rarely, for example, if the mother cannot relax her abdomen enough, the baby is turned under general anaesthesia. If the breech is still presenting at the time labour starts, though—and this occurs in about two in a hundred births—then unless the decision is taken to perform a Caesarian section there will be a breech delivery. The main snags are that the first stage of labour tends to be prolonged; the cord is at risk from compression against the bony pelvis before the baby has been delivered, causing foetal distress; and the head, the largest part of the baby, is born last and has to travel all the way through the pelvis in a much shorter time than in a normal delivery, so that there is little moulding (overlap of the bones of the skull to reduce its diameter) and a risk of damage to the brain from the sudden compression of the skull and the rapidity of its birth. Breech births should always therefore take place in hospital, and forceps are generally applied to the head after the baby has been born, to slow up the delivery and make it as smooth as possible.

One in 100 deliveries results in *twins*. Younger and older mothers are most likely to have them, and the tendency to have twins runs in families. They are less likely to survive than single babies because they tend to be born smaller and complications of birth are more common. *Identical* twins result from a division of the fertilized ovum (egg) into two, from which two identical babies develop. *Non-identical* twins, who are commoner, result from the simultaneous fertilization of two ova (eggs) by two separate sperm, and are no more alike than brothers, sisters, or brother and sister. They have separate afterbirths, whereas identical twins share the same one.

Mothers of twins are more likely to suffer vomiting, and for longer than mothers of single babies; to have a larger womb than would be expected from the date of the last period; to suffer toxaemia and be anaemic; and to go into labour prematurely. The delivery must take place in hospital. The first stage of labour may be prolonged because the muscles in the wall of the womb have been somewhat overstretched. The risk of haemorrhage after the third stage is increased for the same reason, and because the area of afterbirth is greater. Great care is required, if the labour is premature, to see that the babies are not damaged, and this requires often, the use of forceps. The risk of an awkward position of one or other baby, such as a breech presentation, is high.

Since the development of the 'fertility drug', which stimulates the ovary to produce ova, births of two or even more babies have become far more common than they were. The woman who has waited years to have a child is delighted, but bemused to find herself the mother of quadruplets! Of course this is rather too much of a good thing, and as the chance that all such, necessarily, very tiny babies will survive is fairly small, and labour is very likely to be complicated, the pleasure of at last giving birth is soon qualified by anxiety and grief over any babies who do not live. Even if all the offspring do survive, which must give cause for great pride and satisfaction, the physical effort of coping with three or four, or more, very small babies is immense, the requirements for organizing their care are daunting, and the psychological and emotional task of relating all at once to so many new members of the family is likely to be highly complex and perplexing.

10

Lying In

'Lying in' is a somewhat old fashioned term, but I like it! The alternative title for this chapter is the early *puerperium* (puerperium simply means the first six weeks after the mother has given birth) which might seem somewhat discouraging in an informal book such as this. In fact, though, whereas up to twenty or thirty years ago newly delivered mothers were encouraged to take things very easy and lie in bed for a week lest their wombs should prolapse, they are lucky nowadays if they are allowed to 'lie in' for a day.

There are good reasons for this more active and vigorous approach to the early days after delivery. For one thing it is no advantage to the new mother to treat her as an invalid when she isn't. For another, to get her walking about as soon as possible is to reduce the risk of clotting in the deep veins of the legs, which can be serious.

During the first ten days after delivery, which are the most that a woman may expect to stay in hospital, her womb is shrinking, she experiences a variably bloody vaginal discharge called the lochia, and she is getting to know and to care for her baby. The last is far and away the most important, but I shall deal with the other matters first.

The term given to the contraction of the womb to its size before pregnancy is *involution.* As soon as the baby is born the tummy feels remarkably flat, though in fact the top of the womb can usually be felt just below the navel. Within a fortnight however it can no longer be felt through the abdomen, and in two months it is back to its normal size. The *lochia* accompanies involution. The discharge—largely from the site of the afterbirth—is bloody for the first five days, less so for the next five to seven, but persists as a yellowish or whitish fluid for up to six weeks, though it is usually largely over by three weeks. The bawdy say that *sexual relations* should not be resumed before the third stage of labour has been completed—but the more usual yardstick is the ending of the discharge of lochia.

What does a woman feel about the *first sight of her baby*? How long is a piece of string? Some are ecstatic, some indifferent, some (frankly) appalled. Babies are not necessarily beautiful at birth. The moulding of the head produces an unsightly elongation, the caput or swelling of the scalp (due to the pressures of the passage through the pelvis) is unsightly, the vernix or grease with which he or she is covered is hardly attractive, and the red and pink complexion (of white babies) is not altogether becoming. Nevertheless, some happy mothers instantly recognize this as the infant which has been growing inside them for months, and fall in love at first sight. Others are more wary. They are interested, intensely relieved if (as is far more often the case than not) the baby turns out to be quite normal, but do not instantly feel an overwhelming mother-love. Nevertheless they are fascinated by what they have produced, awed and amazed, and determined to do the fullest justice to the miracle of nature in which they have taken part.

Still others may be dismayed by the spectacle of a greasy, blotchy, yelling mite who looks so different from the plump, contented, suckling babies they have seen on the posters in the antenatal clinic, and may wonder how on earth they could be expected to love, or even come to love, such a horrid little thing!

It is said that mothers who witness their babies' births, who are properly awake when they are born and able to take them at once into their arms, recognizing the continuity of the growing being inside them, ever more vigorous as pregnancy advanced, with the 'mewling and puking' infant they now hold, find it easier to love their offspring than those who are over sedated or who have been fully anaesthetized for a Caesarian section, or a forceps delivery, or whose babies are so small that they must at once be removed from them for intensive care. There is evidence that the more contact mothers have with their infants at the start of their relationship the more motherly is their later behaviour. Holding the baby to the breast for a quarter of an hour after the birth has been shown by a Scandinavian study measurably to increase the mother's bonding even months later.

My own research has demonstrated that the average mother is significantly less anxious and distressed immediately after delivery than in pregnancy, and this, presumably, is an indication of the relief she feels once labour is over and she sees that her baby is normal.

The first day after delivery is generally one of rest, recuperation, contentment and immense satisfaction. The memories of labour are likely to be tumultuous—so many thoughts, feelings and sensations crowded into so relatively short a time—the pain and the effort and the uncertainty and the irritation and the excitement and the misgivings, the inevitability and the reactions of others and the baby being born and being seen and being held, and the soreness down below and the thrill and the tiredness and the longing for sleep! During that first day any sense of loss at the baby's having gone from within is offset by pride in achievement and the marvellous novelty of one's own baby, beautiful or not, beside one, with a red wrinkled face and tiny fingers and toes, breathing on its own and stirring and sleeping and unequivocally there, for all to see. Sleep is precious in that first day, and much needed after the exertions of the day or days before, and there are delighted awakenings to the reality of the birth and the baby. Yet it is not always easy for mothers to come to terms with what has happened. The strangeness of having a baby inside one I have already mentioned (pp. 35–6) but over the course of nine months the strangeness fades and becomes familiar and accepted. Then, in the course of hardly more than a day, or even less, the baby is vigorously expelled; the two-in-one has become two persons, so separate that despite the attachments of love and dependency and kinship, if one were to die the other could well go on living. To bring a new being into the world can therefore be sad as well as satisfying. Some mothers feel so close to their babies that it is as if the parting had never happened, but it has. Others feel the need more than once to pinch themselves to make sure they are awake!

The idyll of lying back in justified self-satisfaction, gazing at the baby in awe and joy soon fades somewhat as the pressures of life going on are felt. The baby is not just there to be gloated over or wondered at, but must be fed, washed, cuddled and kept clean. The husband and family, to say nothing of numerous friends, are intensely interested and involved, and the tide of congratulation can be overwhelming. In hospital, the presence of all sorts of other people, staff and other mothers, makes itself felt. The environment is not always congenial, and routines may be resented.

Aches and pains may now be prominent. The breasts feel swollen and a bit sore, it is an effort to pass water or open the bowels, stitches may prick, stretched tissues between the legs smart, muscles never used so fully before ache in protest. Walking is rather painful, but it may be still less comfortable to sit. The womb goes on contracting at odd moments for several days after delivery, especially in women who have already had one baby, causing *after pains*.

So many women experience a fearful sense of anti-climax

on the third day after giving birth that the condition has been given the name *Third Day Blues*.

Delivery is accompanied by changes in the mother's hormone levels almost as dramatic as the departure of the baby from the womb. The high levels of oestrogen and progesterones, and of steroid hormones, particularly those secreted by the afterbirth, fall very precipitately as soon as the birth has been accomplished. It has often been suggested that the Blues (like every other emotional disturbance after the birth) might be due to those hormone changes, or to an alteration in the balance between one hormone and another following the upheaval of delivery.

It is unlikely, though, that the Blues can simply be put down to hormones. Some are inclined to attribute the Blues to the Doctor's loss of interest in the mother once she is safely delivered, claiming that lying-in wards get little medical attention. Probably there is truly an anti-climax, such as is likely to follow the impact of any big or critical change in our lives. The thrill of achievement or good fortune—passing that exam, getting that job, winning that competition—is followed quite rapidly by the realization that life goes on, changes demand adjustment, and that to gain one thing often means giving another up. Yes, the nine months of pregnancy and the hurdle of birth are over. Yes, I've got my baby and he's wonderful/beautiful/at least he's all right/well anyway, I know the worst. But whereas during the pregnancy the baby, even when kicking vigorously, is still more of a potential than an actual being and the relationship between mother and infant, which really makes no demands on the mother at all, is something of a daydream, the born baby, though it has little personality is very real, and if it is not cared for properly it will die. The birth of a baby turns an idea into an actuality and at once there is a major commitment.

First and foremost the *baby must be fed*—but how? Well,

every mother is endowed with breasts, which have enlarged during pregnancy and will get larger still from the fourth day after the birth, as the milk comes in. This milk is a completely satisfactory food for the baby which costs the mother nothing, except that she must take enough nourishment to ensure a good supply. It is always available, without having to be made up, comes at just the right temperature for the baby, and breasts do not have to be washed out or sterilized. Suckling brings mother and baby uniquely close, can give the mother the deepest emotional satisfaction and is a pleasure to those who watch. Yet in Western countries hardly more than a third of mothers *breast feed*. Why is this? Probably because they find breast feeding difficult, distasteful, or a drag.

Difficult: It takes time to establish successful breast feeding. No milk at all flows for the first three days, only a thick yellow fluid called *colostrum*. However, the baby has reserves to keep it going for this time. Still, if it is put to the breast from time to time from the day of birth both mother and baby start to get the hang of things, or at least to become familiar with the situation. At first the baby may not even find the nipple, and may only lick or snuggle when guided to it, but the contact is a stimulus to lactation (the formation of milk) and suckling is still more so. Sometimes the milk arrives before the baby is ready to take enough of it, so the breasts become engorged, hot, tense, and heavy. However, under the guidance of the staff the surplus milk can easily be expressed.

One reason, perhaps, for the decline in breast feeding is the decline in home deliveries. This is not to say that hospitals do not encourage breast feeding, though fashions change. When I was a medical student, mothers in the wards where I was taught were expected to breast feed, and were indeed under considerable pressure to do so. This was often much resented. The staff developed a more laissez-faire, take it or leave it attitude, which was also strongly resented—they should have been giving proper guidance. Now, I believe most units will encourage mothers to breast feed, but in a less earnest and intolerant way than in the days of my youth and without making the bottle feeders feel inadequate and guilty. But, with the best will in the world, mothers exposed to a variety of staff may be subjected to bewilderingly *conflicting advice*. The newly delivered mother may not feel able to discuss the merits of one point of view or another. She may well welcome firm guidance, but gets thoroughly confused when one person tells her very positively that *this* is the way to feed a baby, while another is no less definite that *that* is the way to do it. At home the mother relates to one midwife and one doctor, and things are much simpler.

Although they have no teeth, babies can chew with their gums, and they do! If they chew the *nipples* they will get little milk, feel hungry, frustrated and angry and chew the harder, leaving themselves dissatisfied and the mother sore. The area they need to chew is the areola, or pigmented circle round the nipple, beneath which are little reservoirs in which the milk is stored. By chewing these, and suckling from the nipple, the baby is well satisfied and the nipple is unharmed.

An obstacle to breast feeding may be an inverted nipple. If a nipple doesn't stick out, the baby can't suck from it! Attention to this disorder is required during pregnancy if breast feeding is intended. The use of breast shields in the last weeks of pregnancy is often effective in bringing the nipple out. The ideal hemispherical Western woman's breast is less suitable for breast feeding than some Eastern or African women's more droopy breasts because the baby's nose is flat, up-turned and very near its mouth, so that while it is suckling it may be pressed against the mother and unable to breathe. It is hard to settle down to a healthy feed if you feel that you are suffocating. It is important, therefore, for well endowed women to pinch their breasts between finger and thumb while feeding, so that the baby gets all the areola into its mouth and has the breast held away from its nose so that it can breathe.

There seems little doubt that tension and anxiety can affect not only the production of milk, but the ability of the baby to feed. A tense mother readily communicates her tension to the baby who senses by the feel of her arm, and her breast, an uneasiness that makes him uneasy and fretful too. The anxious mother seeing her baby dissatisfied feels a failure, and a vicious circle is well and truly established. Successful breast feeding requires mother and child to be relaxed and comfortable together. They are more likely to relax, once the rudiments of technique have been acquired, if on their own, or with family or close friends. Such privacy is hard to ensure in hospital, though nowadays most modern maternity units have plenty of little rooms where mother and baby live together, and all at least have bed curtains.

The midwife, whom I have already identified as a key figure at the critical time of delivery (pp. 83–4) is also of the greatest importance in helping the mother to breast feed. If she is rigid, authoritarian and doctrinaire, the mother is likely to feel crushed, anxious or rebellious. Rebellion may well result in her giving up using the breast the moment she gets home. If, on the other hand, the midwife's attitude is casual or indifferent, the mother may well be discouraged. The mother who really doesn't know whether she wants to breast feed or not needs guidance. Even she who is quite certain that she does, but has never done so before, needs some instruction. The helpful midwife will encourage the mother to feed by the breast if she possibly can as there is no doubt at all that breast milk is best for babies (just as cow milk is best for calves!) and that suckling is for many women the most marvellously imaginable form of mothering, greatly enriching the mother-child relationship, and strengthening the mother through the trying times of her child's infancy. The midwife who explains simply and clearly what is to be done, who allows the mother to fumble a bit at first, who is neither hasty nor critical, who supports and encourages in a relaxed, motherly (or at least, sisterly) way, who is careful not to make her feel small or silly, but subtly and sympathetically increases her self esteem, giving her a sense of being capable and sensible and a good mother—such a midwife is doing her job well and has the satisfaction of sending mother and baby off to a flying start.

Sore, or worse, *cracked* nipples will make feeding from the breast exceedingly painful and carry the risk of infection (mastitis) or even abscess of the breast, a very distressing and painful condition. Ensuring that the baby takes the areola and not just the nipple into his mouth (see above) and applying lanolin or similar ointment to the nipples after feeding help to prevent these unpleasant complications. However, if the nipples should become sore or cracked the breasts should have a two to three day rest from feeding. The milk must be expressed, though, by squeezing gently. The sterilized breast milk can then be fed to the baby in a bottle.

The baby may have difficulty in taking the feed because he feels the mother's tension, can't breathe with his nose against her breast (see above) or because he has a snuffly cold, is too little or puny (born prematurely), because of trouble with the mouth or throat—an infection, or a congenital abnormality such as a cleft lip or palate—occasionally because of severe mental subnormality, or because he is generally unwell.

The first two reasons are much the most common.

Distasteful: Most of the aversion many mothers unhappily feel for breast feeding has to do with their sexual significance. A confusion of sexual feeling (or inhibition) with their feeding function causes embarrassment, shyness, anxiety or even revulsion. Women often fear that after breast feeding the breasts will sag and become less attractive. This fear is apparently unfounded: it is pregnancy itself, rather than breast feeding, which can have this effect on the figure, though not commonly, even so, until two or three babies have been born. The use of a supportive brassiere when the breasts are at their largest, in the weeks before and after the birth, is more likely to protect the bust than the avoidance of breast feeding.

Breasts are not only a 'turn on' for men, but a source of sexual excitement for women. To have the breasts touched at all is an intimacy which says that intercourse is likely to follow, a prospect which will please if the partner does. Also, the nipple and areola are highly sensitive erotogenic zones (erotogenic means 'makes you feel sexy'). Under sexual stimulation the nipples become more erect, and various physiological changes have been carefully measured and recorded by the sexologists Masters and Johnson.

Not a few women experience a similar stimulation during suckling, and thoroughly enjoy it. It adds to the sensual pleasure of breast feeding. Others, however, find the feeling disturbing. Sexual stimulation is appropriate from one's sexual partner, but not from one's baby.

Many modest women feel that breast feeding makes their breasts an unwelcome focus for attention from others, and are by no means as free as others nonchalantly to pull out a breast and give it to the baby in company. On the contrary, if feeding at all they will discreetly excuse themselves and put the baby to the breast in somewhat furtive privacy. This is all a matter of how free they feel with their bodies. The work of sex therapists is showing how often women (and men) feel guilty and ashamed about parts of themselves, to the extent of largely disowning nice feelings for fear of nasty consequences—of losing all sexual control, of being seen as impure or bringing down the vague but terrible punishment which the threats and warnings of parents instilled in their childhood fantasies. On the whole, women who are fully at ease with their bodies are most unlikely to suffer any problems with sex or breast feeding.

Some women, though unaware of any sexual stimulation, regard breast feeding as degrading, reducing them to the level of primitive peoples who know no better, or who have no other means of feeding their infants, or even of animals. They think of the sheep suckling the lambs, the calf at the cow's udder, and shudder! Who wants to be a cow? Likewise, the woman who resents her biological role, wanting to be free to be a person without the physical handicaps of her female reproductive physiology (for whom the curse really is a curse) will have no time for breast feeding. She has been irked and oppressed enough by the long nine months of pregnancy and isn't going to extend the baby's physical dependency on her alone by breast feeding, when by choosing the bottle she ensures that anyone else can give a feed if she is otherwise engaged.

The thought of having a baby nuzzling, suckling, and biting at the breast is not simply distasteful to a few women, but alarming. It is not so much the use of the breast that disturbs them as the idea that the infant is taking sustenance from their body. These mothers find little lovable in their newborn child but, on the contrary, view him with apprehension and misgiving, as an alien creature, all powerful in its helplessness, who will take them over, and drain them dry. These feelings pass as the relationship develops, but they make the early weeks very trying. The mother who sees her baby as a greedy, devouring parasite is psychologically unsuited to breast feed, and it would be harsh and futile to expect her to do so. The use of a bottle enables her to keep some distance between her and her baby until gradually she can get to know, understand and feel for him.

'A Drag': There is no denying that breast feeding is a great tie. This is one of its main attractions for the woman who wants to continue for a while the wonderful feeling of closeness and unity with her baby which she enjoyed during pregnancy. However, it is a heavy personal commitment. The baby has to be fed regularly, of course, whether by the breast or artificially, but nobody else can give a breast feed. (The days of 'wet' nurses are long past.) Now and again a supplementary feed by bottle can replace the breast for one occasion, but the mother's personal responsibility over all is very great, and she may well feel that her life has to be organized round the feeds. She cannot go out for the day unless she takes the baby with her. A weekend away while her mother looks after the baby is out of the question. Four or five times a day she must set aside time for the feeds.

Her husband and other children may feel a bit jealous of so much undivided attention given the baby for breast feeding, and of the peculiar intimacy of the occasion. They may, too, wish that they could give a feed themselves. They might be glad to take the feeding over from time to time and give mother a rest, or more probably, free her for another job they want her to do for them. In hospital time is readily available, but at home there are many conflicting demands and the day is always too short. Consequently many mothers give up breast feeding very soon after their return home.

Having written all this, however, I must say that breast feeding is not the be all and end all of infant care. When it goes well it is highly enjoyable and satisfying for mother and, one presumes, baby, but it has never been shown that bottle fed babies show any significant personality differences from those fed at the breast, nor that they are any more liable to mental disorder or illness. Breast feeding is sometimes a highly emotive cause, which over-enthusiastic advocates have proclaimed with all the fervour associated with others arguing for and against abortion and capital punishment. A woman is not necessarily even a moderately good mother because she feeds from the breast, just as the most loving men and women are not necessarily the sexiest. Nor is a mother by any means diminished as a mother because she uses the bottle. Breast feeding is very nice for those who are successful at it, and all women should be encouraged to try it, because most can succeed. However, there is no need to feel in the least a failure if it is not their choice, or it proves unsuitable now and with this baby (it may not necessarily be so with the next).

Breast feeding speeds the involution of the womb, bringing it more quickly back to its normal size and helps use up any surplus weight gained in pregnancy. It is undeniable that mother's milk is best for babies, conferring certain immunities and eliminating the risk of gastro-enteritis. However, it is also undeniable that the vast majority of bottle fed babies thrive, and there is at least the advantage over breast feeding that the husband and other members of the family can more fully share the agreeable experience of feeding.

A hormone—stilboestrol—used to be given mothers who were not going to breast feed, or who had to stop, to suppress their milk, but the law of supply and demand works so well that if there is no demand the supply soon stops anyway.

Most mothers are eager to *regain their normal weight* as soon as possible after delivery. How soon this will be achieved depends on how much was gained during pregnancy. However, immediately after labour a woman will have lost the weight of the baby itself, the fluid in which it was contained and the afterbirth—about 11 lb (5.5 kg) in all. The volume of the blood is reduced by about 3 lb (1.5 kg) in the next few days by her passing a lot of water, the extra blood needed to supply the baby and the enlarged womb and afterbirth now being surplus. The contraction (involution) of the womb loses another 2 lb (1 kg) by a fortnight after the birth. Mothers who do not breast feed lose an extra 2 lb (1 kg) as their breasts return to their size before pregnancy (breast feeders have to wait until weaning for this). So a weight loss of 18 lb (9 kg) or so is rapidly achieved. If, however, the mother has over-eaten during pregnancy, either because her appetite was too good for her calorie requirements, or because she felt miserable or upset and consoled herself with food, the fat will stay unless she diets.

Regaining the normal weight is also part of regaining the *normal figure*. This also depends, though, on getting the well-stretched muscles of the abdominal wall back in tone. During the period of involution of the womb the tummy rapidly gets smaller, but the final return to flatness may well depend upon exercises. The breasts, as has already been mentioned, may sag a little after two or three pregnancies. A somewhat unwelcome consequence of repeated pregnancy is *stretch marking* on the skin of the abdomen, which can only be lessened by plastic surgery.

There is a lot of *water to be passed* in the first few days after delivery, and should there be an infection of the bladder or kidneys (for instance, because of the use of a catheter) this will be painful. However, the use of an antibiotic will soon clear the infection up. Likewise, constipation can be a problem, because any straining may aggravate soreness in the tissues around the vagina, especially if there has been a tear or an episiotomy, and a gentle laxative may be required for a short while.

The *stitches* of an episiotomy will be removed on around the seventh day after birth, or if catgut has been used they will be absorbed and need not be taken out at all.

Now that women get up to go to the lavatory and are walking about to talk to other women almost as soon as they have had the baby, the risk of clotting or *thrombosis* of the veins of the legs is much less than when they used to be kept in bed for a week.

A thrombosis of the visible veins which can be seen and felt as a line of hardness and inflammation in a superficial vein is less dangerous than a deep thrombosis, which causes swelling of the leg and pain in the calf. The danger is that a piece of the clot might break off and be carried by the blood stream to the heart and then to the arteries to the lungs and block them. This condition called *pulmonary embolus* can be fatal, and to avoid it, should a deep vein thrombosis develop, anticoagulants are often given for a while, reducing the clotting tendency of the blood.

A hundred years or so ago *puerperal fever* was a terrible scourge of women who had just had babies, with an appallingly high mortality but in modern obstetric practice it is uncommon and easily controlled. Causes include infection of the womb, associated with retention of a piece of the afterbirth (which can also cause bleeding later in the lying in period if it does not do so straight after the third stage of labour); infection of the perineum, which will only occur if there has been a tear or episiotomy; urinary infection and breast abscess.

If a mother has her baby in hospital how long should it be before she *goes home*? The shortest stay is six hours, the longest usually ten days. The shorter period is obviously for women who simply want the safety of a hospital birth and once delivered, want to be home as soon as possible. The more usual short stay, though, is for two days, which allows the mother a day to recuperate and another in which to gather herself and her baby together before she departs. The longer stays of a week to ten days allow the mother much more time to get to know her baby and how to feed, change, bath and cuddle him. While in hospital she can really be relieved of all other tasks, which is harder to ensure at home. On the other hand she may be distracted by resentment of hospital restrictions and routine, confused by meeting so many different members of staff, irritated, embarrassed or upset by other mothers, or she may be very homesick. She is in a good position to learn exercises to restore her figure and put the pelvic muscles back in tone (important for preventing prolapse and constipation, and for making love!), and about sensible dieting. Above all she is enabled to get plenty of rest which, without having to be bed bound, she badly needs. She has been through a lot, and has a lot yet to go through. Lying in is a good time for lying in!

11

Homecoming

If she has been in hospital for a week or more there is hardly a woman who is not dying to get home. She can't wait to see her husband and family without the restrictions of hospital visiting. She is eager to have her baby all to herself. She longs for privacy and familiar surroundings. She is fed up with midwives, other mothers and hospital food.

Once back, though, and especially when her husband has returned to work and she is for the first time alone, she often finds herself in a state of anxiety. Instead of relaxing and enjoying herself and her baby away from all those irksome hospital rules, she wishes she could have the midwife back at her elbow to tell her what to do now, and reassure her that everything is all right. How on earth is she to get everything done? There's the shopping and the baby to see to, the washing and the baby to change, the cleaning and the baby to feed, the dinner to cook, and, oh dear, why is he breathing like that/crying so loudly/so quiet/so red in the face?

Loneliness and a sense of disorganization are the main problems which beset the newly delivered mother at home. She is so afraid of doing the wrong thing, or that she'll forget or neglect to do what she should. And there simply aren't enough hours in the day. So when the husband comes home he may well find no dinner ready, the baby howling and his wife in tears!

If he is mature and understanding (and he is very likely to understand if he was present at the delivery) he will give her a kiss and a hug and tell her he loves her, and either cuddle the baby while she sees to the dinner, or cook dinner for both of them while she gives the baby a feed. On the other hand, he can make matters much worse by flying into a temper and storming off to a pub.

A great standby to the anxious mother is the *Health Visitor*, a nurse with a special training which makes her an ideal consultant to the newly delivered woman with doubts and fears (which means to practically every woman who has just come home with a new baby). She will call within a very few days (having been notified by the hospital that the mother is now at home) and should not be regarded as an official, a snoop or a busybody, but as an expert and a friend. She knows a great deal about feeding problems, babies' ailments and mothers' feelings. She can supply practical help, sound advice, support and sympathy. She is also to be found at the Welfare Clinic to which most mothers like to take their babies regularly to see that they are thriving and to discuss any problems.

In a small survey I made recently of mothers who had their babies in The London Hospital, I found that of 59 who attended the Post Natal Clinic, only four came home to no help at all. (Such women are, however, in the U.K. entitled to the services of a Home Help, as are those who have their babies at home.) The great majority had their husbands' company for up to a fortnight (though a fifth found them unhelpful) and two-thirds also had support from their mothers or mothers-in-law; this of course was a clientele largely drawn from the East End, where extended families still tend to live closer to each other than in some other parts of the country.

The *mother* or *mother-in-law* can be a great help or a great nuisance. Obviously much depends on the quality of the relationship between mother and daughter, and also on how much the new grandmother can resist getting into the act, and trying to take the baby over. Her own maternal feelings are likely to be aroused by the baby, and strong memories of the time when her daughter was her baby evoked—very probably idealized by nostalgia. She may well feel a little jealous, and may have pronounced views on the way things should be done. If the other grandmother is around and has equally pronounced but different views, then tension can mount till the young mother wishes herself well shot of both of them.

The good grandmother loves the baby, wants to help out all she can, is eager to babysit, but recognizes that her daughter (or daughter-in-law) is a mother now, and wants to do everything she can to see that she does the job well. These remarks apply mainly, of course, to the birth of a first child. When others come along the grandparents are of the greatest value in looking after the other children.

The *husband* whose attitude when his wife comes home is, 'thank God that's over now, perhaps things will get back to normal' is going to be disappointed. At first his wife is very preoccupied with the baby, and other tasks are unlikely to be performed very well unless he does them himself. He may or may not get an ecstatic welcome when he comes home from work but he is unlikely always to find a tidy, well-stocked house, a placid, well-fed baby, a receptive ear when he off-loads the day's frustrations, his dinner cooked and a wife eager afterwards to haul him off to bed. He may well indeed find the place a shambles, no food in the house, let alone cooked, a yelling baby and a weepy, scratchy wife who only wants to go to bed to sleep for ever, leaving him to cope with everything. The immature, dependent husband, or the male chauvinist pig who feels that having the baby is her business, but he still comes first, can, as has already been mentioned, make matters very much worse. I believe that the seeds of marital breakdown can be sown at this time. It takes two to tango, two to make a baby, two to make light work of pregnancy and labour, and two, certainly, to cope with the offspring, particularly in the first weeks and months. And if one opts out, the other will find this hard to forgive.

Although, in general, *anxiety* seems to subside remarkably once the birth is safely over, *the baby* is a source of infinite worry to the more nervous and insecure mother. He seems so small and helpless that anything could carry him off. He has to be protected from her carelessness, ignorance or the effects of her half-acknowledged feelings of disappointment and rejection: in an unguarded moment she might neglect something vital or do him a mischief. She may feel she does not really deserve him, having been so bad and jealous a daughter and wife, and so she may lose him.

Such a mother is never relaxed and only briefly reassured. If she is breast feeding she worries that she may be giving too little; if bottle, that the mixture is incorrect, or unsuitable. She worries when the baby sicks back his feed, worries over the colour and consistency of the bowel motions, worries about *wind*. The baby swallows some air when he cries and if he gulps greedily when feeding and this distends his stomach so that he feels rather full and won't want to take much more of the feed until he has got rid of the air by belching or burping. We ourselves do this quite often during the day (discreetly or noisily according to our temperament) and have no problem because we are normally upright and the air naturally finds its way up. Babies however are horizontal when they feed and therefore need to be sat up from time to time to let the wind escape. And that is all there is to it. There is actually no need to jog them or rub their backs, though it may be rather fun to do so. If the wind comes up with a noisy burp then it is obvious that it has done so, but it may make its exit more silently. Winding should be quite a jolly business but anxious mothers can make rather a grim ritual of it. Incidentally, any patent medicine advertised to bring up the wind is most unlikely to do so more effectively than simply sitting the baby up.

Bringing the feed back is often a consequence of too

much wind in the stomach, and an indication that feeds should be more leisurely, with more time for sitting up. The *motions* for the first few days are normally greeny-black. This is the meconium, present in the foetal rectum (which is passed when there is foetal distress). They then become quite soft and yellow, and it is quite normal for them to be passed several times in a day, though some babies on the breast may go two or three days without passing any at all. If motions are infrequent but soft when passed, and the baby appears well, there is no cause for worry about constipation, which is indicated by a hard motion, passed not very often, and for which the doctor or Health Visitor's advice should be sought. The doctor's advice should also be obtained, speedily, if the motions are green and runny as this (especially if there is vomiting too) may indicate gastro-enteritis.

Babies who *cry* a lot, especially at night, worry most mothers. They cry if they are hungry, in which case they need a feed; if they are uncomfortable, when they may need winding, or a nappy changed; or if they are frightened, cross or sad, in which case they need a cuddle. However, the mother who is tense when she cuddles instils her own anxiety into the baby, who then struggles and howls the more, making his poor mother wonder what on earth she can do, until perhaps the child is worn out, or someone more relaxed takes over. The infant who yells at night may be hungry, angry, wet or scared, but may also be bored. Not every baby needs to spend every hour of the night asleep, and some may badly want to be picked up and played with. This is all very well from their point of view, but not from that of the weary parents who have had one wearing day and need their sleep before facing another. The mother may well feel very torn between her desire to comfort her baby and her yearning to get her head down. How to resolve this is a very individual matter, but it can be said that babies do cry because they want attention, may cry for more when they have been given it, but after a spell of noisy protest will settle down after two or three harrowing hours without it. This being said there are a few relentless cry babies, who may need the doctor's advice on sedation, less for their own sakes than their distraught parents'. Of course, sick and ailing babies cry because they feel ill or in pain, but are less likely to be pacified by being picked up and should show other signs of not being well such as vomiting or a temperature.

If perforce the young parents are staying with the mother or the mother-in-law, problems of a crying baby are likely to be aggravated by the intolerance of the older generation, who may mutter about having had enough of that when you were a baby, thank you very much, and may insist on interfering. Similar protests from neighbours or landlords, particularly in flats, can make life very difficult for the young mother; even if she were prepared to let her baby cry himself to sleep rather than pick him up again and again through the long night, others may not let her do so.

Then there are mothers who worry because the baby *sleeps* too soundly; has he perhaps become unconscious and unrousable? If he is very quiet indeed, is he dead? So there is a great temptation to wake him up to see that he can be woken, which probably won't please him overmuch.

Anxious mothers worry about the baby's *weight*. After losing a few ounces of birth weight in the first few days, babies normally gain seven or eight ounces (210–240 grams) every week for the first three months, and then slow down somewhat. However, they do not have to put on this much every week. Sometimes they gain steadily, sometimes by fits and starts, so that what is not achieved this week is likely to be accomplished by a spurt in the next or the week after. There is therefore no cause for concern if the weight remains static for a week or so provided the baby is contented and appears well. It is a good idea to confine weighing to the Welfare Clinic. This goes especially for the technique of weighing the baby before and after a breast feed to see how much he has taken. The anxious mother weighing the baby every five minutes at home is likely to work herself up into a panic. In the Clinic the job is done accurately and the result can be interpreted reassuringly.

The trouble with newborn babies is that they can't talk. They can't even smile, though when bloated and windy they may seem to do so. They cannot directly reassure the troubled mother that she is doing well and that they feel happy and loved and satisfied. True, they are likely to cry if they are not, but an absence of crying is not enough to put the more uncertain mother at her ease. The baby senses her unease and is made fretful by it, each unsettling the other in a vicious circle only interrupted by a confident husband, a comforting grandmother, a sensible neighbour or a calm and knowledgeable Health Visitor, who will step in for a moment, respond to the baby's evident thriving and give reassurance in a matter-of-fact, 'of course, he's doing all right, isn't he beautiful?' way.

It is an enormous relief for these mothers when at the age of four to eight weeks (or occasionally earlier) the baby can smile. As he grows to recognize the difference between himself and the world about him, there is constant feature in an often bewildering environment, his mother. And he smiles at her. She smiles back, delighted at his recognition, and he smiles the more broadly, and blows bubbles, and waves his arms and legs, and she is delighted; this is the moment she has been waiting for. The baby now feels safe with her, knowing that she looks after him, whatever her mood, and she basks in his approval. This is so often the happy ending to the apparently interminable vicious circle of the anxious mother and the anxious baby.

Before this state of relative bliss is reached, there is hardly a harrassed mother who has not, at some moment of extreme stress, felt so desperate and distraught that she has wanted to throw her baby out of the window, or smother him, or hit him very hard indeed. Such feelings are frightening and disturbing. No mother feels entitled to them, few do not feel wicked, unmotherly and unnatural for having them. They are afraid to speak of them, expecting others to recoil, shocked, and take the child away. They realize that they are being totally unfair. The baby is a helpless little creature with the most limited and rudimentary grasp of its situation, and control of its behaviour. It cannot possibly be judged bad, or wilful. Yet mothers can feel persecuted by them beyond endurance—raging little monsters who can in no way be satisfied but shriek their demands so relentlessly that the only solution seems to be to stifle them.

Mothers who have not yet developed a strong love for the baby are more liable to such frantic *aggression*, but even the most loving are not exempt. Mothers who actually batter their babies are but a very small proportion of those who feel like doing so; the impulses are essentially the same, but for reasons I will discuss a little later (p. 143) they act upon them. Such hostility is far more easily endured if only it can be shared and talked out. The Health Visitor in particular knows that this is a common enough feeling and that a woman is neither a freak nor a monster if she experiences it. She can help the woman gain a perspective on her problem and relieve her guilt and her fear that pent-up frustration and anger may erupt in violence.

If there are *other children* their reaction to the new arrival must be taken into account. As the mother swells during pregnancy there is a natural opportunity to introduce some of the facts of life by explaining that the baby is inside and placing the child's hand over the womb, so that he can feel his soon-to-be little brother or sister kicking. If the birth takes place at home the child feels less excluded than if the mother goes away to hospital, and although he should be kept out of the way during the actual delivery, by a grandparent or a good neighbour, he can see the baby straight afterwards. It may be best to make the introduction to the infant in its cot or crib, rather than in the mother's arms, so that there is a less immediate challenge from a possible rival. The child is bound to be intrigued, but not necessarily captivated. He may not like the look of the baby, not necessarily because of jealousy but because newborn babies are not all that beautiful in the eye of every beholder. However the fact that the tiny being is there at all is a wonder and the mother can show her other child or children the fascinatingly miniature parts of its body without demanding an instant joyous acceptance. If she asks, 'isn't he/she lovely?', the child is in a quandary if he doesn't find the baby lovely at all. Either he lies and says 'Yes' and feels uneasy, or he says 'No' and may be in trouble; so the new relationship is off to a shaky start. It is best to let him develop his feelings in his own time before requiring an expression of them.

Hospital deliveries are necessarily more stressful to the child left behind or sent off to Gran's. A young child does not like to be without his mother in the first place, and when the absence ends in the production of a baby he can easily feel angry, dismayed, even betrayed, and displaced. Though the same principles for introducing the infant to its big brother or sister apply as at home, hospital is a distractingly different, disturbing and mysterious place. It may help if the child has been to the antenatal clinic with his mother once or twice, and it is certainly desirable that he has ample access to her during the lying in period. Even so, it is not easy for him to sort out his feelings about the new baby from the strangeness of the whole situation. Why is mother in hospital anyway? Why can't she come home now?

Jealousy of the new little brother or sister or *sibling rivalry* is inevitable, and needs tactful handling. Sooner or later curiosity and excitement give way to the awareness that this addition to the household is neither a toy nor a pet but a little person of considerable standing, fully the equal of the other children and commanding a good deal more attention.

'Mother I'm tired of my little brother', says Humphrey Devize in Christopher Fry's *The Lady's Not For Burning*, 'will you please give him away to some charity?' Most mothers understand why their children should be extra demanding when confronted by life with the newcomer, and dig deep into their reserves of love to respond, realizing that to be irritable or rejecting from time to time is natural but unhelpful; after all it is unlikely that the child was consulted before the baby was conceived, so it is hardly fair to require him to be wholly welcoming!

Getting into a routine is an important technique for adjustment to life at home with a new baby. The routine cannot be the same as before the birth, as the more rigid obsessional women are likely to find to their cost, but must be modified to the needs of the newcomer. Priorities must be established; people come before polishing! It is essential to feed the baby, but even if this is on demand rather than every so many hours a certain rhythm and regularity are likely soon to be established, so that the day becomes more predictable; after all, most of us having eaten lunch do not immediately feel like tucking into dinner. It is a good idea to have one room (as well as the kitchen) reasonably clean and tidy, for visitors and as an occasional haven from chaos, and to cope with the rest of the place as and when the opportunity affords. The houseproud woman who feels insecure and disgraced if her home is not always spick and span, scrubbed and swept and polished and dusted till it seems presumptuous actually to live there, will wear herself to a frazzle if she tries to keep up those standards in the puerperium, especially as she expects that she is expected to make her baby just as spick and span and 'a credit' too. The slut (Katharine Whitehorn's use of the word gives me leave to follow her) whose untidiness falls just short of actual squalor has a far easier time of it, though it helps to be reasonably tidy and to know where things ought to be.

However full the day, it is very important for the mother, especially in the early weeks, to set some time aside for *rest*. She does not have to mollycoddle herself, but it is no good her slaving all day to collapse dog-tired at night, struggle out of her sleep to deal with the baby's demands through the night and then wake in the morning feeling like a zombie. I exaggerate a little perhaps, but only to make the point that a cat-nap during the day, particularly in the afternoon when the baby has just had a feed and the home may be relatively quiet, can be worth two hours' sleep at night. It is not self-indulgence, but common sense. Thus refreshed, the mother feels quite ready to face her taxing world again. 'Never miss a chance of getting your head down' might well be a motto handed to every woman by her midwife as she leaves her to cope with her baby.

Between six to eight weeks after giving birth, the mother should attend the hospital or her general practitioner for a *postnatal examination*. The main purposes of this are to check that things are returning to normal, to remedy those which are not (e.g. anaemia, urinary infection, piles, high blood pressure) and to give advice for the future (contraception, genetic counselling). At the same time the baby should be examined (see next chapter). Some mothers default from the postnatal clinic, which is a pity. It is an excellent opportunity to meet the midwife again and discuss the inevitable worries of the first few weeks. There is also the chance to meet the other mothers, compare notes and show off the babies. Advice on any continuing vaginal discharge, resumption of sexual intercourse (if not already resumed!), the return of periods and when, if at all, to have another baby is available.

I have remarked earlier (p.19) that in the period after having a baby a woman is particularly at risk of *psychiatric illness* and as this has been my research interest, I should like to mention this now. I am aware, though, that in this chapter I have already dealt more with the difficulties than the delights of the puerperium, so I will try to redress the balance somewhat by stating that most women suffer no psychiatric disorder at all at this time, that severe breakdown is relatively uncommon, and that the outlook for any mental or emotional illness developing after childbirth, be it severe or mild, is very good.

The Puerperal Psychoses are serious mental illnesses, most likely to occur when there is a family or previous history of such disorder. They probably follow one in 200 births, and lead to admission to a psychiatric ward after one in 500 births. The main forms are melancholia (severe depression) in which the mother feels totally unworthy and has impulses to kill herself and her baby; mania, where she is extremely cheerful and confident, and feels that her baby's needs will be met by a 'lick and a promise'; schizophrenia, when she is dreamy, withdrawn, odd, and again liable to neglect her baby; and paranoia, when she feels others are plotting harm to her or her baby. Delirium, which accompanies such severe disorders as puerperal fever and eclampsia (fits following toxæmia) is now rarely seen in the West.

The outlook for all these forms of mental illness is good. Most are over within weeks. Drugs and electroconvulsive therapy to combat depression, tranquillizers for mania, schizophrenia and paranoia, and psychological support are the main treatments. If the mother is not too disturbed she may be treated in the lying in ward or at home, under close supervision by the family doctor, health visitor or community nurse and psychiatrist. If, however, she is admitted to a psychiatric ward she can often take the baby with her and this is of great help in establishing a satisfactory relationship between mother and child.

The risk of relapse after having another baby is about one in seven. Doubtless this is so (relatively) low because the first signs of recurrence are promptly treated.

Far more common, though, than these serious forms of mental breakdown, and to my mind far more important, are states of *depression* intermediate between the mild weepiness of the 'Blues' (p. 101) and the total despair of the fortunately infrequent melancholia. One in ten women, by the time of her postnatal examination, has not achieved a happy adjustment to her new way of life, but feels decidedly low, tearful and dissatisfied with herself. She is not like this all the time but bad days outnumber the good. She may feel all right when she wakes, but as the day wears on she gets more and more miserable, irritable, weary and unable to cope. Usually she eats poorly but may stuff herself in a depressive way for consolation. She snaps at her husband, smacks her other children, feels like shaking or throttling the baby when she cannot pacify him, and is thoroughly ashamed of herself. She worries endlessly about the baby, in the typical anxious mother's way, and worries about her own health too—is she anaemic, is her heart all right, has she some glandular disorder, or cancer? When she goes to bed the last thing she wants to do is make love; all she craves is sleep to bring oblivion and restore her energy, but she finds she cannot drop off.

His wife's depression makes considerable demands for tolerance, support and understanding on the husband, to which he may not rise. Finding that since giving birth she has become tired, unhappy, irritable, inefficient, has let herself go and is disinclined for sex, he may well feel fed up and put out, especially as she cannot really explain why she is in such a state. If he reacts to her unsympathetically she will feel worse, miserable, inadequate and resentful, and the seeds of marital breakdown may be sown (p. 114, 115).

In my previously mentioned research, having identified a group of women who had developed this *neurotic* form of puerperal depression (neurotic means the same sort of thing that you and I get, only worse, whereas psychotic disorder, psychosis, is outside normal experience) I compared them in many ways with a group of women who were not depressed. There were surprisingly few differences. Although, according to a personality test, the depressives appeared significantly more introverted and anxiety prone, it may have been that their depression distorted their answers to the test. Certainly they were no more likely to have been depressed or anxious in the past, except, perhaps, after the birth of a former baby.

Women feel very much on their own with this depression, because they cannot understand it. What reason is there to be depressed? They have come safely through pregnancy and delivery, have a normal healthy baby, which everyone says is lovely, and yet they feel miserable. How can they be so ungrateful and unmotherly? They do not feel that the depression is an illness which they could justifiably take to a doctor. In any case, they have probably heard that everyone gets a bit depressed after having a baby, so presumably they are making heavy weather of what other women cope with quite easily.

If such a mother is asked, say at the postnatal clinic, if she has felt depressed since the birth she is quite likely to say 'Yes' and to burst into tears. These tears express not only her distress, but her relief at being asked. After all, if the doctor or midwives can ask such a question, they are recognizing that depression happens, as a problem is worth talking about and possibly can be treated.

And, indeed, it can. The first step is for the mother to be 'allowed' the feelings she has tried to disown because they seem so awful. This the midwife, in particular, can do by encouraging the mother to talk of her unhappiness, her anxieties, her sense of failure, and her flashes of hostility without scolding, deploring, interrupting or even reassuring, but quietly listening until she has had her say. Time is at a premium in the postnatal clinic, but this is time well spent. Next she can explain that this form of depression can happen to anyone, though it does not afflict everyone it affects quite a few, so she is not utterly alone in feeling as she does. She can then be reassured that sooner rather than later her depression will lift and she will then find herself enjoying life as before and, as a bonus, her baby. If she seems to be stuck, her doctor may prescribe an antidepressive and, perhaps, a tranquillizer which will hurry her return to normal. And until that time it will always help to share her trouble by talking her feelings out, seeing them in perspective, and being reassured of the distinction between emotions and actions (it is one thing to feel like throwing one's baby out of the window, another actually to do so!) in discussion with her doctor or health visitor.

Having stated this, I should acknowledge that there are some women who appear not to make a full recovery from this form of depression, but are left with some symptoms which persist for a year or more. I shall have a little more to say about these in the final chapter.

12

Babies in Trouble

In this chapter I shall consider the mother's and the father's feelings about the *abnormal baby*. The disorder may be prematurity, illness, congenital abnormality of varying severity, stillbirth, or early death. The parents' feelings depend partly on their personalities and any previous experience of such problems, and to a great extent on the nature of the abnormality, its severity and the outlook. For instance, the concern for a previously normal baby desperately ill with gastro-enteritis is very different from that over a physically fit child with severe mental handicap.

A baby is regarded as *premature* if it weighs less than $5\frac{1}{2}$ lb (2.5 kg). Usually, but not always this means that it has been born several weeks early. If however it is small but born around the 40th week its chances of survival are improved. About one in 14 babies born in the U.K. is premature.

Social factors are important; lower social class and living standards, poor antenatal care, illegitimate pregnancy and teenage motherhood all predispose to prematurity. Toxaemia, anaemia, diabetes and kidney disease in the mother and the presence of placenta praevia or twins are also associated.

A premature delivery is usually, of course, unexpected, quick and easy because the baby is so small. The bones of the skull however are soft and easily injured, so forceps are frequently used to protect it.

Premature babies are not only small, but more wrinkled and less chubby than mature newborn infants. The head is larger in proportion to the body, the eyes always closed. They suck, breathe and cry rather feebly, and sleep a lot. They are less immediately attractive than normal babies, looking sometimes like wizened little old men, or baby monkeys.

Being immature and lacking body fat they are at great risk from chilling and must therefore be kept in an incubator, with a special oxygen supply as breathing is often inefficient. Feeding is a problem in those who cannot suck, and feeds may have to be given, little and often, down a fine tube passed down the nose and into the stomach. Extra special precautions must be taken against infection.

Consequently the mother's physical contact with the baby is at first much reduced. However, those majority who survive (the chances being the greater the heavier the baby and the nearer to term its time of birth) are usually able to leave hospital at a weight of $5\frac{1}{2}$ lb (2.5 kg) and will then develop so as to be indistinguishable from normal babies.

The mother has to contend with her shock and dismay at the early birth, her concern over the evident frailty and feebleness of the baby, the realization that it may not survive, the separation when other women are cuddling, feeding and getting to know their babies, and the disappointment of returning home and having to leave the infant for a while in hospital. There is a sense of failure in having produced so small a baby too soon, and the guilt which is so easily aroused whenever anything goes wrong with childbearing comes to the fore. 'What did I do wrong?' or, 'this is my punishment'. Anxiety is extreme and continues well after the baby has come home, there being a nagging doubt that having made so shaky a start he must be damaged and will not thrive. Deprivation of normal contact may hamper the development of mother love, but not necessarily; some mothers feel an intense yearning protectiveness to their very little one in its artificial womb, even though the moment of reunion is postponed. Others, however, being afraid of their grief should he die, shut off their feelings and defend themselves against attachment. Still others are frankly depressed, fearing the worst.

Good antenatal care, an improved general standard of living and contraception and the increase in terminations of unwanted pregnancies in single adolescent girls have reduced the frequency of premature births in the developed countries, and the highly skilled care now available in hospital, obstetric and paediatric units has greatly increased the premature baby's chances of survival. By keeping the mother very well informed, letting her see her child very often and tend him as soon as possible, keeping up daily contact even after she has left the hospital while the baby remains there, she is greatly helped, but special allowance needs to be made for the extra anxiety she is likely to suffer for quite a few months after taking him fully into her own care.

The great majority of *illnesses* to which small babies are subject are trivial, but cause the anxious mother considerable alarm and distress. Nappy and so-called heat rashes, cradle cap, sticky and watery eyes, feeds that are brought back and bowel motions of a funny colour are commonplace, and easily dealt with. Colds make the baby wretched, especially as he cannot feed very well with a blocked nose (and doesn't know how to blow his nose!), but they pass. If the baby becomes chesty though, or develops a sore throat or earache, he will need an antibiotic from the doctor.

Some babies are a bit yellow (*jaundiced*) on the third day of their lives, and this is normal. A serious form of jaundice, however, afflicts some *Rhesus babies*, and can cause brain damage. The mother's blood is in a different group from her baby's, and she develops an immune response (somewhat similar to the rejection of organ transplants) and antibodies to the baby's red blood cells, which are therefore broken down in large numbers, causing anaemia and the jaundice. This is a serious state of affairs, which may require early induction of labour and transfusion of the newborn baby. The immune response builds up through successive pregnancies, and the level of antibodies is monitored during pregnancy, so that everyone knows what to expect and how to deal with it. All the same it can be a harrowing crisis, especially for the mother, bringing a sense of urgency and emergency to the delivery and the fear that the baby will die or be permanently damaged. However susceptible mothers can now be protected from sensitization by their baby's red blood cells by being given an injection of antibodies just after delivery, and this has greatly reduced the frequency of Rhesus disease. Also, modern techniques are so refined—it is sometimes even possible to transfuse the baby in the womb—that the chances of healthy survival of a Rhesus baby are now very high.

Gastro-enteritis has killed many babies, and made many others very ill. It is a very serious infection of the stomach and intestines, causing vomiting so severe that the baby keeps little if anything down, and watery diarrhoea, so that not only food but water and vital electrolytes are lost. As the infection is usually taken in by mouth, gastro-enteritis is unlikely to occur in a baby exclusively breast fed. Contamination of a bottle feed is the usual cause, which emphasizes the importance of hygiene in preparing the food and keeping the bottle and teat germ-free. Some highly infectious forms of gastro-enteritis in hospital have caused epidemics. The sick baby needs treatment in hospital, isolated from other children, until shown to be free from infection and able to keep feeds down. Until then fluid is given by a drip into a vein along with an antibiotic. Needless to say parents suffer anguish and self-reproach and the pangs of being separated from the child while he is so desperately ill as to be beyond their care.

Fits cause great alarm, both at the time they are occurring and by what they are thought to imply. The baby suddenly loses consciousness, all the muscles of the body go rigid first, then jerk quite violently and there is then a brief period of inertness when, especially as he is by then a nasty blue colour, he may be thought dead. Next, however, deep breathing restores the colour to a healthy pink and consciousness returns. As a first aid measure it is important to make sure that the air passages are clear by turning the baby on its tummy, turning the face to one side or the other and removing any food from the mouth. While it is desirable to have the baby seen by a doctor as soon as possible, it is probably best not to rush him off in the throes of a fit but leave him where he is till it is over; the main danger of a fit is choking. Usually a fit is a single occurrence in a baby and does not signify epilepsy but a high temperature, which needs to be brought down by junior aspirin, sponging and treating any underlying infection.

The term *failure to thrive* covers a wide variety of disorders which prevent the baby from developing as rapidly as he should. He may *not be getting enough milk*, or the mixture may not suit him. The mother may not have enough breast milk and in countries afflicted with widespread poverty and famine there may not be the wherewithal for bottle feeding. Occasionally the mother is simply not giving the baby sufficient, because of ignorance, low intelligence or rejection (see 'Non Accidental Injury, p. 143). The baby may be sucking poorly because of immaturity associated with prematurity or mental handicap, or because of a sore mouth (e.g. infection with thrush) or a mechanical problem such as a cleft palate.

Having been swallowed, the milk may *stay in the stomach too long* (a condition called pyloric stenosis causes serious delay, most of the feed being vomited back, and requires an operation at, typically, three weeks old) or may *not be absorbed properly* from the intestines. Among the various causes of this, most of them congenital, are fibrocystic disease (cystic fibrosis) which affects the lungs as well as the pancreas, an organ essential to normal digestion; coeliac disease, which becomes apparent when the baby is weaned on to cereals, and is due to sensitivity to one of their ingredients, gluten and must be treated by a gluten-free diet; and 'milk allergy', which may be a true allergy to a protein in cow's milk, and does not therefore affect breast-fed babies, or may be carbohydrate intolerance, when certain sugars in milk (breast as well as cow's) cannot be absorbed.

Constipation, if severe, causes diminished appetite and some degree of intestinal obstruction. Excessive *fluid loss*, from sweating in an overclad baby, or in a hot room or a hot house, can cause constipation. Some cry babies cry so much that they lose excessive moisture from their lungs, with a similar effect; thus we can see how the emotional disturbance in an unhappy or unsatisfied baby can directly cause failure to thrive. In the forbidding sounding Hirschsprung's disease there is constipation from the moment of birth because of a defective nerve supply to the rectum.

Various *diseases* less closely connected with the intestines can also prevent the baby from thriving—congenital heart and kidney disease, chronic infection of the lungs and kidneys, some tumours of the brain, and certain disorders of the metabolism.

Some babies *only appear not to thrive* being naturally small, in consequence of a low birth weight or their parents' smallness, and having only a small appetite, gain weight slowly. This does not, of course, mean that they are unwell, but anxious parents can create a problem, as they can aggravate that of genuine failure to thrive, by pressing the child to take more than he wants. This he is likely to vomit, which is not very pleasant for him, and the more worrying to the parents, and thus a vicious circle can be set up. A baby truly failing to thrive needs careful assessment by doctors; most often the problem will be found in the feeding. But a small, slow growing but healthy baby simply needs to be allowed to grow at his own pace.

Babies are sometimes born with *marks* of a rough passage into the outside world. The caput or swelling of the scalp, bruising of the face or scalp, a black eye, the marks of forceps blades, even paralysis of one side of the face due to pressure from the forceps, or a fracture of the collar bone are all more or less unsightly but clear up completely very soon. *Birthmarks* are not, in fact, birthmarks but congenital moles, or collections of tiny blood vessels beneath the skin. Most disappear soon after birth, some stay the same, some enlarge, and can be disfiguring. Guilty or fearful ideas about wicked thoughts, the evil eye or physical injury in the womb producing the birthmark are common, but merely superstition.

Severe *birth injury* to the head, of which breech and premature babies are particularly at risk, can cause bleeding within the brain and death or subsequent spasticity. Most *spastics* however are congenitally so, the abnormality developing, for reasons little known, while the baby is still in the womb, and causing both physical and mental handicap. In *spina bifida*, which results usually in only physical handicap, the vertebrae over the lower part of the spinal cord have failed to develop properly, the site of the deficiency being covered with a hairy mole. The spinal cord, without its normal protection, is easily injured and paraplegia, incontinence and paralysis of the legs, results. The condition can be diagnosed in the womb by the presence of an abnormal protein in the (amniotic) fluid in which the baby lies. Down's syndrome (*mongolism*) can also be diagnosed in the womb by the presence of an extra (23rd) chromosome in the cells from the foetus which float in the fluid. Mental handicap of varying severity, a very characteristic (and rather endearing) physical appearance and frequently some degree of physical handicap, such as heart abnormality, are the manifestations of Down's syndrome. It is more likely to occur in the babies of very young mothers and those over forty. *Deafness* is a physical handicap which can seriously retard intellectual development, especially if undiagnosed; German measles during the mother's pregnancy is one cause. From the moment of birth babies can respond to loud sounds; the Moro reflex in which, in response to a loud clap, the baby throws out his limbs and then draws them right in, can be used to test the hearing. *Phenylketonuria*, a rare biochemical disorder causing mental handicap, the effects of which are lessened by putting the baby on a special diet, is diagnosed by a blood test as part of the routine examination of the new born. Further assessments are made at the Postnatal Clinic, periodically at the Infant Welfare Clinic, and when the child goes to school.

There is everything to be said for making the *diagnosis of handicap* as soon as possible, so that any appropriate early treatment can be given, special management planned and above all so that the parents are put fully in the picture. Genetic counselling on the risk of any subsequent offspring is also required.

The *reaction* to a handicapped child is one of shock, dismay, disbelief, depression, guilt, fear and, often, anger. The realization that there is something seriously wrong with the baby which can never be put wholly right, the dashing of hopes of a shining future, and their replacement with the prospect of an endless, shameful burden is truly shocking. Disbelief is a characteristic early reaction to many catastrophes—'this can't be happening'—anger a later one—'why should this happen to us?' Disbelief may develop into denial—'there's nothing wrong with my baby, there can't be, I won't believe it!' However, depression is a more usual response to the realization of the unhappy fact. Depression ranges from prevailing sadness to overwhelming misery and a sense of futility and total inability to cope. Yet again there is guilt, a feeling of being found out and punished, a mortifying sense of failure which transcends disappointment, deep shame, a wretched awareness of being incomplete. Guilt contributes to a compulsion to atone by doing the very best for the hapless infant, devoting one's life to his care. Fear may have a similar effect—one must strive to do one's utmost lest still worse befall. On the other hand fear may be paralysing—after such a heavy blow all confidence is lost and the least action is fraught with unexpected disaster. This is one of the reasons why the baby may be rejected. Another is revulsion. The attempt to identify with what is seen as a monster is so disturbing that there is a turning away and an urgent need to put the creature out of sight and, it is hoped, out of mind. Anger contributes to this rejection too—anger with fate, with God, with the doctors, anger of each parent with the other, and their respective families for carrying the taint which caused this terrible thing: all is displaced on to the afflicted baby, which is then harshly spurned—'What's it good for? Let the State look after it. Better still, let it die!'

The question of how much effort should be put into keeping seriously handicapped newborn babies alive is a difficult ethical one. Quality of life is clearly a most important consideration, as are the parents' wishes. It seems hypocritical to have a liberal attitude to abortion and a strongly protective one to life after birth. Actually to kill deformed babies might be the thin end of a dangerous wedge, but that is a different matter from strenuous resuscitation and surgery which facilitates life of a sort, while leaving grave disability. Yet there have been individuals who were helped to triumph over appalling handicaps, notably Helen Keller, who could neither see nor hear but became a sensitive writer.

If the parents choose to keep the handicapped child they need counselling from the doctor and social worker about the problems that will arise, the child's potential, and about the facilities—medical, social, educational—which are available. They need, too, the opportunity to air their feelings frequently. Peter Nichols' marvellous but harrowing play, *A Day in the Death of Joe Egg*, shows how the parents of a severely handicapped little girl escape from their anguish and despair by the use of sick humour, inventing a personality for their mute, helpless and unresponsive child. Where there are other children there is a danger that they will be neglected while every care is lavished on the weaker little brother or sister; such care is sometimes a compensation for guilt and hostility, sometimes given in the totally unrealistic expectation of improvement. While the parents of severely handicapped children may not be much more liable to mental breakdown than those of normal offspring, the strain may show in their marriages.

Parents need help to come to terms with the crisis of their first reaction, to talk of their subsequent misgivings and to take a reasonably optimistic but realistic attitude to the challenge which confronts them. They must be allowed their moments of bitterness and despair, and the situation at home needs to be kept under review so that action can be taken, such as placing the child temporarily in care, if the burden is clearly becoming too oppressive. This said, it is happily true that for not a few parents the care of the handicapped child is not a heavy duty but a pleasure. Mother-love can be a formidable power in looking after the lame duckling.

Stillbirths are slightly below one hundred times less common than live births. Causes include insufficiency of the afterbirth for various reasons, severe abnormality of the foetus, Rhesus incompatibility and very occasionally snagging, twisting or knotting of the umbilical cord. When the baby is dead no movements are felt (though normal babies may be inactive for as long as a day), there is no further weight gain (in fact some may be lost) and the breasts shrink to their usual size; in fact the woman no longer feels pregnant. If the heart cannot be heard even with an ultrasonic detector, and there are the characteristic X-ray changes which occur three or four days after the death, the diagnosis is confirmed.

The doctors then have the job of telling the mother, and it must be said that they do not often do it very well, though to break such bad news well is extremely difficult. Sometimes the evil day is postponed, but the mother's reaction to the realization that she has been carrying a dead baby inside her for not just days, but weeks, may be one of horror. Usually the doctor will want to tell the father with or before his wife, and away from the hurly-burly of the antenatal clinic. Not only has the mother to cope with the loss of her baby, but she has to go through the ordeal of labour before she can work out her grief. She is usually anxious to get the birth done with, and though on obstetric and medical grounds it can be argued that she should wait until she goes spontaneously into labour, for humanitarian reasons induction is to be preferred. The labour is a sad, subdued affair, truly a labour, which everyone wants to get over with as soon as possible. The lifeless infant is bundled away to an anonymous disposal. Doctors and midwives are awkward and embarrassed, not knowing what to say. In the hospital the mother feels herself shunned. No one likes to broach the subject of her loss, and the contrast between her lot and that of the mothers with live babies is too painful for all. It is a relief to let her go to the emptiness of her home.

Some mothers try as quickly as possible to conceive,

and if successful are extremely apprehensive during the next pregnancy, though the birth of a live normal baby usually seems to make up for the previous loss. What has been lost is one who might have been, rather than one who was, and keen as the grief and disappointment are, they are not generally irreparable. Other women, if childless, may be put off childbirth by the experience and throw themselves back into their careers. Many change their doctors.

The Muslims (like the Roman Catholics) believe that the foetus has a soul, and if stillborn should be buried with full rites. It has been suggested that if this were a more general practice, and if the parents could see their dead baby before its burial in a named grave, their loss would at least be dignified and rendered more tangible.

The *death of the newborn baby* is felt more as the loss of an actual person, and later deaths more so still. Premature and very abnormal babies are especially at risk. Death in the first week of life is about as common as stillbirth. The first babies of women over forty and, interestingly, the third babies of women under 20 are most at risk. A particularly tragic and mysterious loss is the *cot death*, in which an apparently healthy infant, usually between two and four months old, dies suddenly, nearly always in his sleep, and post-mortem examination shows no cause. About one in 500 babies die this way and the impact of the loss is the greater because of its mysteriousness. Self-searching, blaming and a terror at the arbitrary vindictiveness of fate are common reactions.

To end this chapter I should mention that there are several excellent comprehensive and well-informed books now available to parents on the development and disorders of infants which are a mine of good sense, reassurance and practical advice on how to cope. While I wish to record my own debt to Dr Benjamin Spock's altogether admirable *Baby and Child Care*, there are now other works of comparable merit well worth tracking down.

13

Back to Normal?

In this final chapter I shall deal briefly with the readjustment necessary during the first year of the baby's life. The '?' in the title indicates firstly that, anyway with the arrival of a first child, things never go *back* to normal—the past when the parents were just a partnership is gone for good—and secondly, that things do not always go *on* to normal, but some difficulties may develop and persist through this year and some times for years afterwards.

My favourite example of the difference between good and not so good *mothering* is given by the psychiatrist Gerald Caplan. He describes a woman faced with a pile of ironing, while her toddler is on the floor nearby playing with building bricks. The good mother notices that her child is getting very cross and frustrated because he cannot make a pile of the bricks. So she stops the ironing, even though she has plenty to do, and gives him some time, showing him how to make the bricks stay on top of each other. She recognizes his need and meets it. The other mother, however, is ironing away while the toddler is playing very happily. She feels sorry for herself—she is such a drudge, there's no end to the work and where is her husband? Probably away somewhere having a good time. All she's got to love her is her own little boy. Overwhelmed by self-pity and longing for comfort, she stops ironing, rushes across the room, sweeps her little one up in her arms and hugs him close. And he struggles, wanting to get back to his bricks. She is using him to meet her own needs.

Does good mothering matter? Immensely, I'm afraid. John Bowlby, an English psychiatrist who has made a life study of the attachment of the child to its parents, has shown that the ability to make affectionate relationships in adult life depends very much upon the experience of mothering.

Spoiling a baby is not a matter of over-indulgence. No baby was ever made into a selfish, demanding adult by being picked up and cuddled too often when he cried. The truly spoilt person is one who felt insufficiently loved in infancy and who consequently keeps demanding attention and gratification when 'grown up'.

Anxious, insecure, dependent people are very likely to have had parents who did not respond to their appeals for affection, or were actually rejecting; to have been without a parent for long spells, sometimes through being put in a hospital or Home; to have been threatened with withdrawal of love, or abandonment, as a means of control; to have heard the parents threatening to leave or kill each other, or themselves; or to have been guilt-ridden by warnings that misbehaviour would make either parent ill, or bring them to an early grave.

Mothers like the woman who picks up her child to give herself comfort may martyr themselves to their children as a means of securing their love. They turn the normal relationship upside down by making their children feel excessively responsible for them. Such children are liable to be afraid of going to school, and to be *agoraphobic* (afraid of leaving home) as adults. A form of personality disorder in which the person cannot tolerate frustration of his demands, will use violent or criminal means to get what he wants without learning from past experience or heed for the future, cannot sustain a relationship, can only use and abuse other people and feels no love, guilt or remorse (the *psychopath*) is significantly associated with prolonged deprivation of maternal care in the earliest years of life and subsequent rejection by parents or foster parents.

Depression at all ages is significantly associated with the loss of the mother, through death, sickness or desertion, in young children. The 'stiff upper lip' supposedly characteristic of Britain (or more particularly, the British middle class), which indicates a defence against feelings and reluctance to admit any need for other people, is another consequence of a love-starved childhood. Strict, severe, controlling, punishing parents are likely to produce *obsessional* offspring, conscientious and methodical but afraid of their strong feelings.

The quality of mothering and parental care in childhood thus has a considerable bearing on the kind of spouse, parent, indeed citizen the adult becomes, and so emotional deprivation can be passed on from one generation to the next. 'Non Accidental Injury' is now the official term for the more emotive *battered baby*. Only relatively recently have doctors and social workers become aware that babies and young children with bruises, broken bones, who are underweight and somewhat backward in their development, may be victims of their own parents' violence and neglect. Several studies have now shown that such parents differ from those who only *feel* like bashing their offspring (the majority!) in that they require a loving response and self-control from the baby long before the normal age. Having been deprived of mothering in childhood and treated more harshly, they are more likely to favour corporal punishment and its early administration. (Battering, however, is not like an ordinary smack or spanking, the parent loses his or her temper and hits, punches or kicks the child really hard.) They are inconsistent in being sometimes harsh, sometimes lax, sometimes loving, often not. They tend to be young, to have conceived before marriage, and quite often the mother is living with a man who is not the child's father.

A minority of 'battering' mothers are suffering from depression. They feel very guilty about the loss of control and are likely to seek help because of what they have done. This help, taking the form of regular close support and antidepressive drug treatment, is usually very effective.

Otherwise, 'battering' parents are unlikely to tell the truth, and may even persuade themselves that the explanation they give for the baby's black eye and the burn on his knee is what really happened. Few do not want to keep their child, and fear of losing him causes evasiveness and downright lying. They may not feel much guilt because they feel that they were provoked, or were using normal parental control, though they are usually dismayed at having gone so far. They are not wicked but troubled, insecure, find life a struggle and feel very much on their own. However, they can be very dangerous to their child. Battered babies are distinctly at risk of being beaten to death. The harm to the child of being parted from parents he usually still loves (children rarely see themselves as victims, but are sorry to be so bad) must be set against the risk to life and welfare if he stays at home. Close supervision by doctors and social workers is vital. It has been well said that this is 'an area in which social, medical and legal action must be authoritative, intrusive, and insistent', but at the same time it should be constructive.

Essential to good mothering are the provision of *emotional security* and encouragement of the child to *explore and develop* as a separate person. The good mother recognizes her baby's need for love and consistently meets it, so that in later life he feels a loved and loveable person, worthwhile and able to give love to others. She also recognizes that he is not a part of herself any longer, but a separate being, born at a different time into the world with a different heredity and needing to extend himself through relationships with others, within and outside the family, and by exploring his world with the curiosity which characterizes our species. Children given the security of love and the freedom to explore grow up stable and self-reliant, trusting and helpful to others. Bowlby reports that rather more than half of the child population appears now to be brought up this way.

Mothers who are very motherly and love their baby from the start may have more difficulty in allowing him to be separate, a unique individual in his own right, than those whose maternal affection develops more slowly and who from the beginning regard the baby as somewhat different and 'other'. In the course of bringing up a baby, as during pregnancy, old conflicts are revived, and there is the chance of finding a new solution which leaves the mother a more secure and mature person than she was before. In weaning, say, or toilet training her infant there is an echo or overtone from the mother's distant past which may trouble or challenge her; in coping successfully she takes her second chance and lays some old ghosts. Between the ages of three and seven months the baby is easily enjoyed and presents few problems. He is attractive, responsive, recognizes his mother and smiles at her, generally contented, giggles and chuckles and develops most interestingly week by week. Towards the end of the first year, however, he is starting to show independence. He can stand, crawl into all sorts of mischief and may start to walk. Advanced babies may even begin to talk. He has some teeth and is able to bite. Conscious control over opening bowels and passing water is developing. He is becoming aware of his father and the other members of the family. All this progress is very exciting, but some mothers may feel a pang as they recognize that when the baby stands on his own two feet he is doing just that!

As far as husband and wife are concerned, foremost among things which should go 'back to normal' is the *sex life*. This may have been restricted in the later weeks of pregnancy and will certainly have been during the first month after the baby's birth. The husband is likely to be eager, but the wife may be more wary. For one thing, she may be very much *afraid of conceiving again.* If the labour was an ordeal she is in no hurry to repeat it. If she has had several children, she may want no more. In any case, she is unlikely to want to conceive another child before her baby is a year old. The Dutch cap may not fit properly before the womb has involuted fully, a coil will not have been fitted yet, she may be uncertain about the use of the Pill before the return of periods, and neither she nor her husband may have much faith in withdrawal. Under these circumstances, it is best for the man to use a sheath. Its use takes some of the spontaneity out of love making, but it is reliable and readily available. However, so as not to cause his partner any discomfort both the sheath and her vagina should be lubricated with a jelly, oil or cream. Obviously any worries about contraception should be dealt with as soon as possible; the postnatal clinic gives an ideal opportunity.

Pain is another reason why women do not enjoy sexual relations after childbirth. This may be a result of tension and anxiety, or a temporary consequence of the repair of an episiotomy incision, which can result in tenderness at the back of the vagina. Pain during intercourse can easily cause tension, increasing the pain. The liability to pain is much eased by lubrication, and by the man's exerting the pressure of his penis towards the front rather than the back of the vagina until healing is completed.

Many women in the early weeks of the baby's life feel subordinated to the demands of motherhood. Those who are *depressed* feel like dreary, weary drudges at the end of the day, and far from romantic or sexy. In my survey I found that when they attended the postnatal clinic only 50 per cent of depressives had regained normal sexual interest, compared with 75 per cent of those who were not depressed. Depression of any severity undoubtedly reduces both the interest in and enjoyment of sex, which do not return until the depression has lifted. However, for the woman who feels simply tired, undesirable and bogged down in motherhood, good timing and her man's expertise as a lover can work wonders with her morale. Though not always easy to arrange, love in the afternoons or at weekends, or when the man is a shift worker (or can wangle some time off!) is highly recommended. The lover who is considerate, enterprising, passionate, loving and accomplished can make his wife forget for a blissful half-hour that she is a responsible mother, and remind her that she is still an exciting mistress. The closeness of making love after the baby's birth is an expression of joy in what they have achieved and unity in working together as parents.

Occasionally, of course, there is *no father*. Around nine per cent of births in the United Kingdom are illegitimate, a third of these to mothers under 20 years old. In time of war there are many young widows with children, and many children whose fathers are absent on active service. A woman with a child needs a man, and a child a father or father-figure to support the mother, materially and emotionally, to exercise control and to be a male with whom a growing boy can identify and with whom a little girl can discover how to relate to a man. In the absence of the actual father a substitute may be provided by adoptive or foster-parents, a step-father, a grand-father or uncle or male friends of the family. The woman who tries to 'go it alone' and be both parents to her child is now becoming more common in our society, with the availability of social security benefits, council housing for unmarried mothers and an attitude among more women which favours their independence of men. A marvellous account of such a mother is given by Margaret Drabble in her novel, *The Millstone*. While there is no doubt that the task can be done very well, it is difficult for the mother to be a fully aware person in her own right when she is her child's only support, difficult for her not to feel her life unbearably limited, and difficult for her not too often to use the child to meet her own needs.

A woman does not have to be managing alone to feel cramped and *confined by her maternal role*. Those who had an absorbing and stimulating career can find the simplicity of their new routine at times stifling. Fascinating as babies are, they are no substitute for intellectual conversation. When a woman who was a success in a challenging responsible job finds that her world is now filled with an infant with whom she doesn't cope all that wonderfully well, she can feel diminished and resentful. The quality of the marriage is tested by the ways in which her dissatisfaction can be met. If the husband, at the end of his working day, can take the baby off his wife's hands for a bit, let her off-load her grievances without feeling threatened by them and then steer her gently on to topics other than the baby, and if he insists that they go out for the day or the evening quite often, either fixing a baby-sitter or taking the baby too (so easy while still small enough for a carry cot) he can bring a breath of fresh air in from the outside world, and his wife will feel less claustrophobic. Yet, while it is usually desirable for the mother to be at home with her baby for the first three years some mothers are so discontented that their early return to work is preferable, provided that satisfactory arrangements can be made for the care of the child by day.

George Brown, the sociologist, made a study of depression in a London borough and found that the group far and away most likely to be depressed were young women of lower social class, with children under school age, who were not themselves at work. In my own study of depression after childbirth I found that while 57 per cent of those woman identified as depressed at the time of the postnatal clinic recovered in a matter of weeks or months, 43 per cent failed to do so, and a year later were complaining of such symptoms as loss of sexual and other interests, irritability, fatigue and ready depression. This meant that of one in 25 of all the women surveyed it could be said that that had not been the same since the birth of the baby. No special features were found to distinguish those recovering from those who did not, but the implication of Brown's work is that babies can be a great burden on the mother in conditions of unsuitable housing (e.g., sharing a lavatory, lacking a bathroom, living in a high rise flat) where the husband does not give much support and where there is not the interest and diversion of a job outside the house.

I share with Gerald Caplan, whom I have already quoted in this chapter, the view of childbirth as a *crisis*. This does not mean that it is bad, but big! A crisis is a major life event for which one is not altogether prepared by past experience. It may be a loss, such as bereavement, a gain, such as promotion, or a challenge, such as conception and childbirth. The immediate effect is a state of emotional disturbance, ranging from unease to turmoil, usually lasting a month or two. During this period one is floundering somewhat, anxious, sometimes unhappy, sometimes hopeful, preoccupied with past similar problems, and how one coped or failed to cope, uncertain and generally less efficient and capable than usual. At this time the influence of others is considerable, for good or ill. When the crisis eventually resolves the personality is enriched, unchanged or deprived. To be enriched one has gained confidence and self-esteem and the satisfaction of mastering the crisis and enjoying the rewards. When deprived, however, one is left with a sense of limitation, failure and loss.

As a psychiatrist I may be thought to have a rather warped view of womanhood. Few women consult a psychiatrist because they feel so well and happy! However, in the course of my research I have met, I am glad to say, a majority who were. In my account of feelings about childbirth I should like to claim to be a realist. I have certainly not avoided bad feelings and sad situations. At the same time I recognize that most women cope very well and find giving birth a truly happy event. Most babies are brought up to be physically fit and emotionally secure. It is a great pleasure to watch young children at play in any Western community and see how sturdy, lively and attractive they are. Childbirth is now safer and smoother than ever before.

For those who have dipped into this book, or who are reading it to the end, I trust that it will be an influence for good, dealing with possible difficulties by seeing them for what they are and getting them in perspective, rather than pretending that they are not there.

To finish on a note of encouragement, I ask parents not to worry too much if they don't think they've done a fantastic job. The odd lapse from the best standards is inevitable, and will not ruin a child's future. None of us had a perfect upbringing, as none of us is perfect, but most of us get by. Even seriously disadvantaged children may grow into very successful adults. If we take the trouble to find out what we need to know, and are charitable to ourselves and to our children, we have little to fear and nothing of which to be ashamed.